EXCELLENCE

INSPIRATION FOR ACHIEVING
YOUR PERSONAL BEST

EXCELLENCE

EDITED BY J. PINCOTT

Copyright © 2007 J. Pincott

First published in 2007 by:

Marshall Cavendish Limited
119 Wardour Street
London W1F 0UW
United Kingdom
T: +44 (0)20 7565 6000
F: +44 (0)20 7734 6221
sales@marshallcavendish.co.uk

and

Cyan Communications Limited
119 Wardour Street
London W1F 0UW
United Kingdom
T: +44 (0)20 7565 6120
sales@cyanbooks.com
www.cyanbooks.com

A CIP record for this book is available from the British Library

ISBN-13 978-1-904879-89-3
ISBN-10 1-904879-73-X

Printed and bound in Great Britain by
TJ International Ltd, Padstow, Cornwall

To Peter

Contents

Introduction

The philosopher Immanuel Kant once said, "All the interests of my reason, speculative as well as practical, combine in the three following questions: 1. What can I know? 2. What ought I to do? 3. What may I hope?"

Throughout most of human history, the practical answers to these questions depended on the circumstances of birth: class, race, religion, gender, and geographical location. For most people, personal achievement was unthinkable. They were resigned to know little and hope less, and there wasn't much they could do about it.

Times have changed.

Today, throughout much of the world, the answers to Kant's questions may be, "anything and everything." Anyone has the opportunity to gain knowledge. Anyone may strive to do meaningful work. Anyone may achieve success and fulfillment. In short, anyone may hope to live a life of excellence.

This book is a testament to that goal.

Excellence is a collection of more than 300 insights from remarkable people around the world, throughout all periods of history, and in all fields. Here are CEOs, popes, poets, actors, directors, entrepreneurs, politicians, and others who have made it to the top of their respective professions and have advice to share. Drawing on interviews, autobiographical writings, essays, broadcasts, and other sources, I attempt to get at the heart of what they consider "excellence." In the telling are answers to useful questions: How does one actually achieve excellence? What sort of mindset is required? Who truly leads a life of excellence? What is excellence, anyway?

There are some surprises. Although ambition, persistence, resilience, and risk-taking are the foundation of excellence, other virtues are necessary. True excellence—which goes beyond mere financial and career success—requires you also to be ethical, communicative, worldly, meaningful, and humble. These themes and others are explored here.

Read *Excellence* for inspiration. Flip through the excerpts at your leisure. And as you read, try to apply the famous Kantian musings to your own pursuit of excellence: What can I know? What ought I to do? What may I hope?

J. Pincott
New York

Excellence is an art won by training and habituation. We do not act rightly because we have virtue or excellence, but rather we have those because we have acted rightly. We are what we repeatedly do. Excellence, then, is not an act but a habit.
Aristotle

BEING AMBITIOUS

Excellence depends on ambition, the will to do well. Ambition motivates you to constantly challenge yourself. It's the drive that helps you realize your dream. Have grand expectations—even immodestly high ones—and believe in them. Only when ambition prevails over inhibition is excellence truly possible.

Excellence is the gradual result of always striving to do better.
Pat Riley, National Basketball Association coach

High expectations are the key to everything.
Sam Walton, founder of Wal-Mart

It is a wretched taste to be gratified with mediocrity when the excellent lies before us ...
Isaac D'Israeli, writer

... The world is your oyster ... I grew up thinking that despite the obstacles presented by the swine, I would be successful no matter what I did.
Hunter S. Thompson, writer

Have a goal

What is your greatest vision of yourself? In five years?
Ten years? Twenty? Forty?

Vision is perhaps our greatest strength ... it has kept us alive
to the power and continuity of thought through the centuries,
it makes us peer into the future and lends shape to the
unknown.

Li Ka Shing, *chairman of Cheung Kong (Holdings) Limited and*
Hutchison Whampoa Limited

Ask yourself these questions and answer them honestly: What
do you want? And how will you know when you get it?

People really do have their own solutions. The problem is,
either they don't know how to discover them, or they avoid
discovering them. But if you want to come up with good
decisions for your work and your life, simply ask those two
questions—because it all comes down to very simple things.

Richard Leider, *author, speaker, and counselor*

The man without a purpose is a man who drifts at the mercy
of random feelings or unidentified urges and is capable of any
evil, because he is totally out of control of his own life.
In order to be in control of your life, you have to have a
purpose—a productive purpose.

Ayn Rand, *writer and philosopher*

It was my life's ambition to see a book I had written on a shelf
in a bookshop. Everything that has happened since has been
extraordinary and wonderful, but the mere fact of being able
to say I was a published author was the fulfillment of a dream
I had had since I was a very small child.

J. K. Rowling, *writer*

You need to develop a very clear picture in your mind of how you want and expect to work and live ... The more clarity you bring to the decision, the better the decision will be.

Several years ago, I worked with a man who came to a very clear picture of what he wanted in his life: He wanted to own a sports team. Once that became clear, he worked out, step by step, what it would take to reach that goal: "To own a sports team, I have to amass great wealth. To do that, I have to be an entrepreneur. To do that, I have to learn about running a business—and it needs to be in an industry where there's a great deal of upside potential." As he worked out the logic, it not only made a lot of sense, it also helped guide his decisions.

James Waldroop, management consultant and co-founder of
Peregrine Partners

People ask how can a Jewish kid from the Bronx do preppy clothes? Does it have to do with class and money? No. It has to do with dreams.

Ralph Lauren, designer

Set your ambitions high

The higher your expectations, the greater your chances of excellence in whatever you set out to do.

You know the story of the farmer who in his backyard had chicken, and then he had a chicken that was a little odd looking, but he was a chicken. It behaved like a chicken. It was pecking away like other chickens. It didn't know that there was a blue sky overhead and a glorious sunshine until someone who was knowledgeable in these things came along and said to the farmer, "Hey, that's no chicken. That's an eagle." Then the farmer said, "Um, um, no, no, no, no man. That's a chicken; it behaves like a chicken."

And the man said no; give it to me please. And he gave it to this knowledgeable man. And this man took this strange looking chicken and climbed the mountain and waited until sunrise. And then he turned this strange looking chicken towards the sun and said, "Eagle, fly, eagle." And the strange looking chicken shook itself, spread out its pinions, and lifted off and soared and soared and soared and flew away, away into the distance. And God says to all of us, you are no chicken; you are an eagle. Fly, eagle, fly. And God wants us to shake ourselves, spread our pinions, and then lift off and soar and rise, and rise toward the confident and the good and the beautiful. Rise towards the compassionate and the gentle and the caring. Rise to become what God intends us to be—eagles, not chickens.

Desmond Tutu, cleric, activist, and Nobel Peace Prize Laureate

Don't limit yourself. Many people limit themselves to what they think they can do. You can go as far as your mind lets you. What you believe, remember, you can achieve.

Mary Kay Ash, founder of Mary Kay cosmetics

I always knew I was going to be rich. I don't think I ever doubted it for a minute.

Warren Buffett, investor; chairman of Berkshire Hathaway

Don't limit your dreams. Make them magnificent.

Well I DO want to go up into space, but more than that, I'm dissatisfied with the fact that humans have only gone to the moon. I want to go to Mars! I want to eventually go beyond the solar system!

Takafumi Horie, entrepreneur

As long as you're going to think anyway, think big.
Donald Trump, CEO of the Trump Organization

Start with a dream. Maybe a dream that is personal and small, but worth doing. Then dream a bigger dream. Keep dreaming until your dreams seem impossible to achieve. Then you'll know you're on the right track. Then you'll know you're ready to conjure up a dream big enough to define your future and perhaps your generation's future.
Vance Coffman, chairman and CEO of Lockheed Martin

We want to make smarter search engines that do a lot of the work for us. The smarter we can make the search engine, the better. Where will it lead? Who knows? But it's credible to imagine a leap as great as that from hunting through library stacks to a Google session, when we leap from today's search engines to having the entirety of the world's information as just one of our thoughts.
Sergey Brin, co-founder and president of Google Inc.

I had ambition not only to go farther than any man had ever been before, but as far as it was possible for a man to go.
James R. Cook, explorer

It doesn't matter where you start.

I tell [young people] not to be afraid about starting at the bottom; that they can work their way up; that they need to learn all they can from people who have been in the business longer than they have been. They should be a sponge and just absorb what is going on around them and learn everything they possibly can as soon as they step inside the door.
Katie Couric, news anchor

Us kids in Queens always looked at Manhattan as the Mecca. If you could make it there, you could make it anywhere—that's what Frank Sinatra kept saying. I did 'On the Sunny Side of the Street' because at one point in my life, I realized there was a lot of power in having absolutely nothing. Freedom is either that you have absolutely everything or you have absolutely nothing—anywhere in between, you struggle. So I just decided that I would find that sunny side of the street and be as rich as Rockefeller—or "Gatesefeller" now. To get beyond everything, that's the side of the street I had to choose to walk on.

Cyndi Lauper, singer

When you're a self-made man you start very early in life. In my case, it was at nine years old when I started bringing income into the family. You get a drive that's a little different, maybe a little stronger, than somebody who inherited.

Kirk Kerkorian, president and CEO of Tracinda Corporation

Never settle

You'll never approach anything like excellence if you settle for mediocrity.

Nothing is more sterile or lamentable than the man content to live within himself.
Harold Pinter, playwright, in Tea Party

Success is ... the capacity to dream, and the determination to live in obedience to those dreams. An important but little known American poet, Delmore Schwartz, once wrote, "In dreams begin responsibilities."
Christopher Dodd, US senator

The day we think we've got it made, that's the day we'd better start worrying.
Rich Teerlink, CEO of Harley-Davidson

Ambition never comes to an end.
Yoshida Kenko, writer and Buddhist monk

BEING A COMMUNICATOR

Even entrepreneurs and artists don't work alone. Excellence depends on other people —those who work for you or for whom you work, those who buy what you create, those who support you along the way. The ability to communicate with, reach out to, and inspire other people is crucial. Articulate your goals. Engage others. Make the most of your contacts and support others in their pursuits. Excellence thrives on this synergy.

Under fire, you need to shoot, move, and communicate.
Dean Hohl, *US army ranger*

No-one is big enough to be independent of others.
William Worrall Mayo, *founder of the Mayo Clinic*

I always try to make myself as widely understood as possible; and if I don't succeed I consider it my own fault.
Dmitri Shostakovich, *composer*

Be personable

Use your personality to get others interested in you and working with you.

Charm ia a way of getting the answer yes without asking a clear question.
Albert Camus, *writer*

The most important aspect of my personality, as far as determining my success goes, has been my questioning conventional wisdom, doubting the experts, and questioning authority. While that can be very painful in relationships with your parents and teachers, it's enormously useful in life.
Larry Ellison, *founder, Oracle Corp.*

I have this theory. You know, when they have those polls about the most attractive men, somehow good old Woody Allen always comes out on top. That saves the day for me. He's more consistently up there than someone like Tom Selleck or Don Johnson, who are the traditional good-looking chaps. He beats them because of personality. His sense of humor is far more important than anything else. I probably tend to do better than others because of my personality, rather than my intense good looks.
Phil Collins, *musician*

Humor and charm go a long way.

I think humor is the most effective political tool out there, because people will listen to anything if they're laughing ....
Sherman Alexie, *writer*

Does [anchor Katie] Couric—like most people who are paid a lot of money and enjoy fame and are surrounded by courtiers—sometimes exhibit diva-like behavior? Yes. But she can also conduct a brilliant interview, and is a great mom, and has both humor and charm. Does she throw lamps? No. Do people who work at 'Today' sometimes blame her for tensions on the set? Yes. Does it matter? Only if the audience sees through their television sets that Katie Couric is not what she appears to be: the perfect sister or friend.

Ken Auletta, *journalist*

A sense of humor can help you overlook the unattractive, tolerate the unpleasant, cope with the unexpected, and smile through the unbearable.

Moshe Waldoks, *humorist*

And so does honesty and humility.

If you want to get an audience with you, there's only one way. You have to reach out to them with total honesty and humility. This isn't a grandstand play on my part; I've discovered—and you can see it in other entertainers— when they don't reach out to the audience, nothing happens. You can be the most artistically perfect performer in the world, but an audience is like a broad—if you're indifferent, endsville. That goes for any kind of human contact: a politician on television, an actor in the movies, or a guy and a gal. That's as true in life as it is in art.

Frank Sinatra, *singer*

Force it, even if at the moment it doesn't come naturally.

You've got to get off the elevator each morning with a big smile on your face.

Susan Whiting, *president and CEO, Nielsen Media Research*

If you always go by how you feel, life can end up quite a lonely affair. But if you go against that sometimes—say you're in the middle of an introverted stage and a friend comes for a visit, and you make an effort to get out of yourself, to communicate—I think that's a beautiful thing. It's a sacrifice of your own emotional state for someone else.

Björk, *singer*

Be a leader

No matter your profession or pursuit, it helps to know how to manage others to work toward a common interest. Know how to lead and how to collaborate, and how to balance the two.

Control is not leadership; management is not leadership; leadership is leadership is leadership. If you seek to lead, invest at least 50 per cent your time leading yourself—your own purpose, ethics, principles, motivation, conduct. Invest at least 20 per cent leading those with authority over you and 15 per cent leading your peers. If you don't understand that you work for your mis-labeled "subordinates", then you know nothing of leadership. You know only tyranny.

Dee Hock, *founder and CEO Emeritus, VISA International*

It's a totally collaborative process. I want to hear the crew's ideas. I get the actors to work with the designers on their costumes and sets to make sure that the designs amplify their characters. Then the whole thing just grows. It's very organic. If the actors come up with something more interesting than what I have visualized, that's where we go. I love watching them and being surprised by their moves. I just love good ideas—I don't care where they come from. I work that way more and more.

Terry Gilliam, director

A crucial part of leadership is getting the right people on your side.

The most important thing is to have creative, reliable people.

Harri Kulovaara, executive vice president, Royal Caribbean

Hire people who are better than you are, then leave them to get on with it. Look for people who will aim for the remarkable, who will not settle for the routine.

David Ogilvy, founder of Ogilvy & Mather

You are a bus driver. The bus, your company, is at a standstill, and it's your job to get it going. You have to decide where you're going, how you're going to get there, and who's going with you. Most people assume that great bus drivers (read: business leaders) immediately start the journey by announcing to the people on the bus where they're going—by setting a new direction or by articulating a fresh corporate vision.

In fact, leaders of companies that go from good to great start not with "where" but with "who." They start by getting the right people on the bus, the wrong people off the bus, and the right people in the right seats. And they stick with that discipline—first the people, then the direction—no matter how dire the circumstances.

Jim Collins, management consultant

If you lose great people, you lose success. It's that simple.
Barb Karlin, *Intuit Inc.*

Always recognize the people who help you.

People innately want to be recognized for their hard work.
David Novak, *chairman and CEO, Yum Brands*

Grab them in the gut

Connect to other people with emotions. Get others to see your point of view in a way they can internalize and understand. John Seely Brown recommends using stories and anecdotes to connect to people.

Why storytelling? ... Stories talk to the gut, while information talks to the mind. You can't talk a person through a change in religion or a change in a basic mental model. There has to be an emotional component in what you are doing ... First, you grab them in the gut and then you start to construct (or re-construct) a mental model ... If you can get to them emotionally, either through rhetoric or dramatic means (not overly dramatic!), then you can create some scaffolding that effectively allows them to construct a new model for themselves. You provide the scaffolding and they construct something new. It doesn't seem to work if you just try to tell them what to think. They have to internalize it. They have to own it.

John Seely Brown, *former chief scientist of Xerox Corporation and former director of Xerox Palo Alto Research Center (PARC)*

Developing good communication skills is essential. As governor, I've really learned the value of trying to make sure I'm concise in my message and that people can understand it. While we all have different goals, the objective is the same.
Craig Benson, US governor

The young generation has a different curiosity that is more visual. We coaches have to learn how to deal with that: How do I get to each one best— with a talk, with video analysis? And what sort of tone?
Jürgen Klinsmann, coach of Germany's national soccer team

Learn the art of conversation, the foundation of relationships.

Lockheed Martin embraced "management by walking around"—but the executives didn't know what to say. Well, you say simple things such as, "What's going on with the project?" Show an interest. Be sincere.
Debra Fine, author and consultant

Conversation should be pleasant without scurrility, witty without affectation, free without indecency, learned without conceitedness, novel without falsehood.
William Shakespeare

Know the value of small, personal gestures

In an increasingly digitized world, it means a great deal when you take the time to be kind and develop a personal touch.

Now, let me tell you, I've made a pretty good living off of cellular telephones, but there comes a time when it's time to hang up the phone and get back to talking to people face to face and eye to eye. In today's fast-paced world it's more important than ever, I believe, to do something as simple as remember the good manners that we were taught in the past, simple things like not calling people older than you by their first name unless you're asked, or writing a thank you note to someone when they've done something nice for you, and maybe even using a pen and paper. Taking the time to extend these small personal gestures is a high form of respect.
Mark Warner, *US governor*

Recent studies have found that charisma and kindness matter just as much as – and sometimes more than – credentials when it comes to being hired or promoted these days. A Net Future Institute survey of 223 executives from several different industries found that 63 percent rely on a candidate's "liability" when making hiring and promoting decisions. At 62 percent, "skills" mattered just slightly less.
Kate Jackson, *journalist*

Get others to help you

Improve yourself by bouncing ideas off other people.

I look for bright people with strong personalities who will argue with me. My background is in law and business. I like discussing both sides of an issue, and I'm comfortable with controversy.
Mitt Romney, US governor

You have to let people challenge your ideas.
Tom Kasten, vice president of Levi Strauss and Co.

If you have one idea that you hang on to, you're doomed to suffer. So we started with many ideas and then tested them. Collaboration with others is great if you can listen— which is hard.
Isabella Rossellini, actor

We can believe that we know where the world should go. But unless we're in touch with our customers, our model of the world can diverge from reality. There's no substitute for innovation, of course, but innovation is no substitute for being in touch, either.
Steven Ballmer, CEO of Microsoft Inc.

I believe when you get your goal, you should telegraph it to everyone around you. I would say, "I'm gonna be the strongest man in the world. I'm gonna be rich in America. I'm gonna be the Number One Box Office star in the world." Telegraphing your goal to others makes it real to yourself and it commits you to it.
Arnold Schwazenegger, actor and US governor

31

Focus on helping others, too. It will help you attain a better understanding of yourself and how you fit in.

Instead of imposing your will on every situation, you focus on including everyone else, and just that little adjustment of attitude gives you the space to understand where and who you are.

Wynton Marsalis, *musician*

Network

Every encounter is an opportunity. In a globalized world, you have a tremendous opportunity to benefit from the synthesis of other cultures and perspectives.

More business decisions occur over lunch and dinner than at any other time, yet no MBA courses are given on the subject."
Peter Drucker, *management consultant*

Encounters. When two people meet. Or two particles. Or two cultures. In that crucial moment of interaction the results of an encounter are determined. In the simplest of encounters—say, with two billiard balls—the outcome is a predictable result of position, velocity and mass. But the encounters that interest me most are not so simple. In the encounters of people and cultures, much depends on the path that each has taken to that point ... The encounter has complexity and rich dimensionality. The result of an encounter between two people or between two cultures is shaped by the assumptions of each, by their respective goals ... What makes our current time distinctive are the new combinations of people and cultures that are participating in these encounters.
Aga Khan, *Imam of the Shia Imami Ismaili Nizari*

The implosion of electric technology is transmogrifying literate, fragmented man into a complex and depth-structured human being with a deep emotional awareness of his complete interdependence with all of humanity. The old "individualistic" print society was one where the individual was "free" only to be alienated and dissociated, a rootless outsider bereft of tribal dreams; our new electronic environment compels commitment and participation, and fulfills man's psychic and social needs at profound levels.

Marshall McLuhan, philosopher and communications theorist

BEING CONFIDENT

Excellence requires confidence. Some degree of courage and self-assurance is essential for an extraordinary life. Confidence is not always easily achieved, and even the most confident leaders occasionally falter. Recognizing their doubts and fears as well as finding role models helps successful people overcome obstacles and develop excellence in themselves. Tapping into a common cause—realizing that your effort will help others—is another confidence booster.

Life shrinks or expands in proportion to one's courage.
Anais Nin, writer

Courage is the most important of all the virtues, because
without courage you can't practice any other virtue
consistently. You can practice any virtue erratically,
but nothing consistently without courage.
Maya Angelou, writer and poet

Courage is doing what you're afraid to do. There can be no
courage unless you're scared.
Eddie Rickenbacker, pilot

Underlying the whole scheme of civilization is the confidence
men have in each other, confidence in their integrity,
confidence in their honesty, confidence in their future.
William Bourke Cockran, lawyer, US congressman, and orator

It takes an almost arrogant confidence to do something that
interesting.
Christian Lacroix, designer

Stand on your own

Your best self is your most confident self. Do not be inhibited by those who tell you to "know your place."

It is men and women who have made the world, and they have made it in spite of their gods. The message of the myths is not the one the gods would have us learn—that we should behave ourselves and know our place—but its exact opposite. It is that we must be guided by our natures. Our worst natures can, it's true, be arrogant, venal, corrupt, or selfish; but in our best selves, we—that is, you—can and will be joyous, adventurous, cheeky, creative, inquisitive, demanding, competitive, loving, and defiant. Do not bow your heads. Do not know your place. Defy the gods.

Salman Rushdie, writer

You'll inevitably meet some source of adversity. Have the confidence to stand up for yourself and your principles.

A man who wants to lead the orchestra must turn his back on the crowd.

Max Lucado, minister

You can't build a strong corporation with a lot of committees and a board that has to be consulted every turn. You have to be able to make decisions on your own.

Rupert Murdoch, chairman and managing director of News Corporation

The reasonable man adapts himself to the world. The unreasonable man persists in trying to adapt the world to himself. Therefore, all progress depends on the unreasonable man.

George Bernard Shaw, playwright

Adversity may even inspire you to be more courageous than you would be otherwise.

I was studying at Stanford University. My father suddenly died so I had to rush back to India and I attended the first annual general meeting of my company. A shareholder, who was very articulate, very vociferous and someone who categorised himself as a public spokesman, gave me very sincere advice in front of all the shareholders. He said: "Mr Premji, you should sell your shareholding and give it to more mature management because there is no way a person of your age with your experience can lead this company." And that really made me more and more determined to make a success of Wipro.
Azim Premji, CEO of Wipro

Find role models

We are more similar to one another than we are different. Find role models and learn how those people have achieved excellence in their lives. Imagine they are in your situation. What would they do?

An act of heroism, of extraordinary courage, the grandeur of it, won't easily inspire us to act in imitation, but it can inspire us to emulate its author. For that, we should learn what we can of the whole experience of the subject, the hero's life, as it was before and after, and believe that trying to emulate the character it reveals is one tried way to prepare for the tests that might await us and gain hope that our courage will not be wanting in the moment.
John McCain, US senator

If I am walking with two other men, each of them will serve as my teacher. I will pick out the good points of the one and imitate them, and the bad points of the other and correct them in myself.

Confucius

You don't have to know people personally for them to be role models. Some of my most important role models were historical or literary figures that I only read about I never actually met.

John Wilson, angler and television personality

Whom do I admire? ... Woody Allen. I admire his tenaciousness, his talent, his integrity. I guess what bothers me about saying that is that he's so many people's hero. If I went a step further, I would say John Cheever. His work really touched me. And he seemed to have a very good heart, to have overcome enormous obstacles and achieved success quite late in life. He also wrote about a world that he made me feel I belonged to, even though it had nothing to do with me. That's a great achievement for an artist. I'd say the same about John Updike and Saul Bellow.

Paul Simon, singer, songwriter, and musician

When I see Avril Lavigne or Gwen Stefani or Christina Aguilera on TV, I take pieces from them. I don't copy their music, but I see emotions in their music that inspire me. Instead of girls being like anti-this or anti-that, we should support and inspire each other.

Britney Spears, singer

Family members are often sources of inspiration.

I see myself as about 12. And it's really interesting. My grandmother—what is she, 88? One time, a few years ago, I was looking at her and remembering when she was younger, when I was real little. I remember her wearing cocktail dresses and earrings and gloves, looking real glamorous, even though she wasn't all that young even then. I asked her, "How old do you feel?" She said, "….Even when I see this old, wrinkled woman in the mirror, I still think of myself as being about 17. It doesn't ever really change."

Cher, singer and actor

Acknowledge your fears

Remind yourself that your fears are internal. You choose to let them affect you. Fears must be acknowledged before they can be overcome. Self-mastery is a lifelong process. Many find direction in spirituality.

Mastery of self comes down to the capacity of an individual to discover what it is that they truly want, what their path is, and then to eliminate the obstacles, which are always internal, that would keep them from being able to fulfill that path on an ongoing basis. There are natural obstacles that life offers us in order for us to grow and expand as individuals and discover more of who we are and to unfold more of our spiritual path. But I also think there are a great number of challenges that are self-induced. And we must develop the capacity to meet those, anticipate those as much as possible, and eliminate them by developing what I would consider to be emotional and/or spiritual muscles.

Tony Robbins, management consultant

You must also realize that the stuff of excellence—truth, real scientific truth—can be elusive ... It is too often covered by the heavy fog of fear and hidden by the darkness of your detractors. You must believe in yourself. You must have the desire. You must have the focus to see truth clearly ... As for the second part of the equation, consider it a personal challenge never to let your commitment to learning be denied. To strive for excellence. To believe in yourself and have the ability to prioritize.

Daniel S. Goldin, former director of NASA

Don't be afraid to fail.

There's a wonderful poem by Rainer Maria Rilke that talks about the biblical story of Jacob wrestling with an angel, being defeated, but coming away stronger from the fight. It ends with an exhortation that goes something like this: "What we fight with is so small, and when we win, it makes us small. What we want is to be defeated, decisively, by successively greater things."

Tim O'Reilly, publisher

You can't be afraid of failure, because that's the thing that can scare the hell out of you.

Kate Spade, designer

Try to embrace your anxiety; channel it to work for you.

About half an hour before air time—5pm. That's when I become hyper. I put everything else out of my mind and just let that nervous energy surge through my body. I start talking faster and louder. My confidence comes up. It's actually a great feeling.

David Letterman, talk show host

Cultivate confidence in others

Inspire others to be excellent, too.

Once, at a tennis tournament, I was paired with a woman who had just learned how to play. Every time she missed a shot, she immediately turned to me, expecting that I would be disappointed or frustrated. Instead, I talked to her about our strategy for the next point. By doing so, I sent a very clear signal: The past doesn't matter. I didn't encourage her with empty praise—that approach rarely works. But I knew that if she dwelled on a mistake, she was more likely to repeat it, and that if she focused on how we were going to win the next point, she was more likely to help us do just that. Over several days, her abilities improved dramatically—and we ended up winning the tournament.

Scott Adams, *cartoonist and creator of* Dilbert

BEING CREATIVE

With a little imagination, anything is possible. Of course, imagination isn't confined to the arts. Anyone who has achieved excellence in life—in business, politics, spirituality, teaching, etc.—gets there because he or she has in some way thought differently. Try to be creative in everything you do. Arouse your curiosity. Explore your most outlandish interests.

Tap into your fantasies and ideals.
Let your hobbies inspire your job.
Think up a new way of doing something.
Think of a new something to do.

Excellence is to do a common thing in an uncommon way.
Booker T. Washington, political leader and rights activist

You need chaos in your soul to give birth to a dancing star.
Friedrich Nietzsche, philosopher

The life of the creative man is led, directed and controlled by boredom. Avoiding boredom is one of our most important purposes.
Saul Steinberg, artist

I believe that someone who invents a new category and establishes a system for it is always needed—in every age.
Takashi Murakami, artist

Be curious

Curiosity is the precursor to creativity. Ask "why?",
"why not?" and "what if?".

Curiosity is my mantra. It's also my profession.
Curiosity offers novel lenses for looking at the world.
Tom Peters, *management consultant; co-author of* In Search of Excellence

… Ask high-quality questions, like "What if?" Second,
find people who add new perspectives and create new
conversations … Third, pay attention to those new voices.
If you want unlimited options for solving a problem, engage
the "what if" before you lock onto the "how to." You'll be
surprised by what you discover.
Peter Guber, *chairman, Mandalay Entertainment*

Genius means little more than the faculty of perceiving in an
unhabitual way.
William James, *philosopher*

How do you turn the world on its head?

Listen, it's really pretty simple. If there's a thing, a scene,
maybe, an image that you want to see real bad, that you need
to see but it doesn't exist in the world around you, at least not
in the form that you envision, then you create it so that you
can look at it and have it around, or show it to other people
who wouldn't have imagined it because they perceive reality
in a more narrow, predictable way.
Tom Robbins, *writer*

Cross-pollinate

Expand your repertoire of interests and let each of those interests inspire and inform one another. Peter Drucker once advised a young man keen to know how to excel as a manager, "Learn to play the violin."

To tap the force of imagination, you may have to unlearn as well as relearn. That's what Einstein did. He unlearned the old in order to create the new. Einstein's theory of relativity was a leap of imagination that challenged the orthodoxy of Newtonian physics, and helped pave the way for quantum physics. Quantum physics is not an extrapolation of Newtonian physics. It is a colossal breakthrough in our fundamental understanding of nature. That in turn has spawned an era of new technologies, changing the way we live, work, play and communicate.

Einstein was also a fine violinist. He said, "I am enough of an artist to draw freely upon my imagination ... I often think in music; I live my daydreams in music."

Choon Fong, president of the National University of Singapore

... I thought, "I'm supposed to be an experimental artist? Start experimenting!" I thought if I put myself in really awkward situations, then I'd have some other kind of reaction. So working at McDonald's and working on an Amish farm did that for me. It made me have to think on the spot and improvise, not just fall back on who I thought I was, and what I thought I was supposed to be making, and how I thought people should look at me.

Laurie Anderson, performance artist

Successful businesses can be inspired by drawing on diverse backgrounds and interests.

I've always started businesses. I started a publishing company when I was still in school. And then I co-founded a biotechnology company, which is now on the New York Stock Exchange, called Biomatrix. But I had always been very interested in design, so after about ten years of doing the biotechnology company I was really interested in doing something else.

André Balazs, hotelier

Learn from the creative process

As you build and create, pay attention to the process. Adapt as you go. Enjoy the interplay between conception and realization.

... When you're in the process of creating something ... it's often taking a model that you have in your mind and playing out that model with a new creation in the world. But as soon as you create something in the world, it's not necessarily going to live up to exactly the model that you had in your mind. It will disagree in certain ways or surprise you in certain ways. So by creating things in the world, it leads you to revise the models that you have in the mind. And as you revise the models you have in the mind, it leads you to create new things in the world. So I think that we think about this constant cycle ... taking our ways of thinking about the world and using that

to express ourselves and create things in the world, and
through that activity of creating ... to test out, to try out,
to play with the models we have in our mind and continually
iterate back and forth between the two.

Mitchel Resnick, director at MIT Media Lab

But whether it's evolution or revolution, there's always a better
way to build a computer, or map a genome, or liberate a
country, or take a basketball team to the Final Four. Just work
to understand the world around you. Read books. Read
websites. Read other people. Circle the pitfalls and highlight
the opportunities. Then build a vision of how it could all be
better and work like hell to make it happen.

Michael Dell, founder of Dell Computer

Everyone is capable of being creative, no matter your profession or your specific talents and interests.

Creativity does not require special abilities. Human beings
were born with the ability to create. That's the exact reason
why human beings have created the current civilization.
As I have written in my book, some people achieved something
when they accidentally exercised creativity at the right time.
Other successful people may have been well aware of what
creativity is and exercised it right. The difference between
successful and unsuccessful people is whether they exercised
their own creativity or not.

Koichi Tanaka, Nobel Prize Laureate in Chemistry

Look at the familiar in a different way

You might find inspiration in unexpected places.

... I was flipping channels one night, and there was a program about Harry Partch—you know, he made up all this insane music in the 50s, on these instruments of his own making. And on this program there was this beautiful orchestra playing these crazy instruments, playing 'US Highball,' this amazing oratorio by Harry Partch. And they were all dressed like bums. It was just beautiful to look at, and to listen to. So I thought, "Oh, my God, look at these bums, they're so elegant." And I do that every time I see a bum. But there was something about this particular bum with the orchestra next to him, something beautiful about the contrast of the bum and the elegance. So I thought, my Fall collection has to be bum-ish, right? So I came into work and told everybody and they were like, "You're crazy."

Isaac Mizrahi, designer

I am never more alive intellectually or emotionally than when I am, for example, sitting outside of a yurt in Mongolia listening to a young nomadic tribesman describe how he rode his horse 20 miles through freezing temperatures just for the chance to vote. Or sleeping in a cargo container as I did just this spring in the Pakistan earthquake zone with young American relief workers who had been on duty there for three months. Or riding a humvee with American Special Forces through a hot combat zone in Afghanistan to a primitive village to make sure people have the medical needs that they desired and needed. Or stepping into a wilderness anywhere in the world with all that I need in a backpack, no call waiting, thank you very much.

Tom Brokaw, news anchor

Different ways of seeing are what make life interesting.

… Take any piece of land. Let alone the farmer and the real estate agent or the picnicker, one painter will see it flat, another painter will see it in depth, another as structure, another as fluffy, another as dark and light, another as spots and lines, another as still, another as changeable, another as full of detail, another as a general expression or mood, and so on. But it is all the time the same commonplace piece of land. Likewise people and ideas are normally just as commonplace, but they are irregular since they do contain what is from the practical point of view an excess of aspects and qualities. If it were not for this excess nobody probably would go on living, because in it is all possibility and all novelty and all freedom.

Gertrude Stein, writer

BEING DISCIPLINED

Without discipline, excellence is fleeting.
Excellence requires focus, the ability to focus
and to create for oneself a sense of structure.
Discipline is the dray horse of excellence:
it means will power, self-sacrifice. It requires
a long-term outlook. Paradoxically, discipline
can be liberating. It shapes your identity,
it provides a sense of ritual, it gives you
the freedom to build.

If you do not conquer self, you will be conquered by self.
Napoleon Hill, writer

Without discipline, there's no life at all.
Katharine Hepburn, actor

Get into situations in which failure isn't an option.
Francis Ford Coppola, film director

Self discipline is that which, next to virtue, truly and
essentially raises one man above another.
Joseph Addison, politician and writer

Be your own master

Learn to channel your energies. Every successful person will attest: Self-discipline is essential for excellence.

In reading the lives of great men, I found that the first victory they won was over themselves ... self-discipline with all of them came first.
Harry S. Truman, US president 1945–1953

No horse gets anywhere until he is harnessed. No stream or gas drives anything until it is confined. No Niagara is ever turned into light and power until it is tunneled. No life ever grows great until it is focused, dedicated, disciplined.
Harry Emerson Fosdick, clergyman

When man learns to understand and control his own behavior as well as he is learning to understand and control the behavior of crop plants and domestic animals, he may be justified in believing that he has become civilized.
Ayn Rand, writer and philosopher

I never could have done what I have done without the habits of punctuality, order, and diligence, without the determination to concentrate myself on one subject at a time.
Charles Dickens

Talent without discipline is like an octopus on roller skates. There's plenty of movement, but you never know if it's going to be forward, backwards, or sideways.
H. Jackson Brown, Jr., writer

Hold yourself responsible for a higher standard than anybody else expects of you. Never excuse yourself. Never pity yourself. Be a hard master to yourself-and be lenient to everybody else.

Henry Ward Beecher, clergyman and reformer

Self-discipline is what happens backstage every big success.

Most of the time I take [my work] dead seriously—to the point where most people find me kind of tiresome, I think. Not that I care. It's just because I always believe it can be better, and I always strive to make it better. I always feel like it's a living thing, and you should treat it as a living thing. I don't think it's a product that should be delivered and finished and tied up, like it can be quantified, like it can be understood. People used to make fun of me for getting to the theater early and preparing, always being there hours ahead of time. It's not like it was work; I just love it. There's no place I'd rather be.

Mary Louise Parker, actor

Reduce bad habits

Be prepared to make small sacrifices for true excellence. Eliminate bad habits with self discipline.

Excellence is an art won by training and habituation. We do not act rightly because we have virtue or excellence, but we rather have those because we have acted rightly. We are what we repeatedly do. Excellence, then, is not an act but a habit.

Aristotle

Men are anxious to improve their circumstances, but are unwilling to improve themselves; they therefore remain bound. The man who does not shrink from self-crucifixion can never fail to accomplish the object upon which his heart is set. This is true of earthly as of heavenly things. Even the man whose object is to acquire wealth must be prepared to make great personal sacrifices before he can accomplish his object; and how much more so he who would realize a strong and well-poised life.

James Allen, writer

Every one of us is going to have to work more, read more, train more, think more. We will have to slough off some bad habits—like driving gas guzzlers that weaken our economy and feed our enemies abroad. Our children will have to turn off the TV set once in a while and put away the video games and start hitting the books.

Barack Obama, US senator

The individual who wants to reach the top in business must appreciate the might and force of habit. He must be quick to break those habits that can break him—and hasten to adopt those practices that will become the habits that help him achieve the success he desires.

J. Paul Getty, founder of Getty Oil

Use props to help discipline yourself

It may be useful to make up rituals to help you focus.

I write until the first draft is finished, and then I feel that I can get out. But, during the time of the writing of the first draft, I don't go out. I'm just locked away, writing. It's a time of meditation, of going into the story. You know, I feel that there's a dark space, and I go into that dark space where the story is. And I just have to show up every day with a candle, and slowly, it will start to unfold ... It's a real candle, but it's also a metaphysical candle ... I don't like clocks. And if I have a candle, for as long as the candle is burning, I write. And then, when it's over, when it burns off, I can have dinner and get out, and do things.

Isabel Allende, writer

If I'm not at my desk by 4am I feel like I'm missing my most productive hours. In addition to starting early, I keep an antique hour glass on my desk and every hour break briefly to do push-ups, sit-ups, and some quick stretches. I find this helps keep the blood (and ideas) flowing.

Dan Brown, writer

Commit to a routine

Develop good habits. Discipline yourself to an allotted amount of time each day to focus on your goal.

I did figure out that I tended to write good stuff first thing in the morning. So I had all this free time in the rest of the day that I had to occupy with something other than writing. Because if I sat and wrote, I'd just bury the good stuff I'd written in crap and have to excavate it later. I did some construction work with a friend of mine. Basically, the work habit I developed out of all that was of setting things up so I could write in the morning and then stop and exercise my penchant for getting into the nitty-gritty details of physical things. Not because that was productive in any way but because it kept me from screwing up whatever I happened to be writing. I tried to pattern things that way ever since.
Neal Stephenson, writer

I am building a fire, and every day I train, I add more fuel. At just the right moment, I light the match.
Mia Hamm, US Olympic football player

When a person trains once, nothing happens. When a person forces himself to do a thing a hundred or a thousand times, then he certainly has developed in more ways than physical. Is it raining? That doesn't matter. Am I tired? That doesn't matter either. Then will power will be no problem.
Emil Zatopek, Czech Olympic gold medalist in long distance running

Control your emotions

A significant part of self-discipline in the ability to control your anger and frustration.

I think the guys who are really controlling their emotions ... are going to win.
Tiger Woods, golfer

... The mark of the good loser is that he takes his anger out on himself and not his victorious opponents or on his team-mates.
Richard Nixon, US president 1969–1974

Just as your car runs more smoothly and requires less energy to go faster and farther when the wheels are in perfect alignment, you perform better when your thoughts, feelings, emotions, goals, and values are in balance.
Brian Tracy, talk show host

Make a lifelong commitment

Make excellence sustain for a lifetime. Maintain good habits and values for the rest of your life.

Nobody's a natural. You work hard to get good and then work to get better. It's hard to stay on top.
Paul Coffey, athlete

Something in human nature causes us to start slacking off at our moment of greatest accomplishment. As you become successful, you will need a great deal of self-discipline not to lose your sense of balance, humility and commitment.
Ross Perot, founder of EDS and Perot Systems; US presidential candidate in 1992 and 1996

Your ability to gauge your success will largely depend on how you perceive it. How you choose to perceive it is entirely up to you. Your perception of this intangible ideal called success is something you can control. You can shape it, set it up, feel it, and define it. Allow competition to turn inward. If you do not depend on awards, money, or other validations to dictate your well-being and your measure of success, you will own your happiness.
Jonny Moseley, skier, Olympic gold medalist

The unfortunate thing about this world is that the good habits are much easier to give up than the bad ones.
W. Somerset Maugham, writer

BEING
ETHICAL

The world needs excellence. In an era of corporate scandals and widespread corruption, being ethical is in itself a form of excellence. Ethics are relevant on every level. Be aware of all the big and little social contracts you make with others, and don't break them. Improve the world as you improve yourself. Adhere to a moral code or vision. Do the right thing. You might realize that the better you treat the world, the better the world treats you.

A man's ethical behavior should be based effectually on sympathy, education, and social ties; no religious basis is necessary. Man would indeed be in a poor way if he had to be restrained by fear of punishment and hope of reward after death.
Albert Einstein

When I do good, I feel good; when I do bad, I feel bad, and that is my religion.
Abraham Lincoln, US president 1861–1865

The remarkable thing is that we really love our neighbor as ourselves: We do unto others as we do unto ourselves. We hate others when we hate ourselves. We are tolerant toward others when we tolerate ourselves. We forgive others when we forgive ourselves. We are prone to sacrifice others when we are ready to sacrifice ourselves.
Eric Hoffer, writer and activist

Have a moral vision

Excellence embraces a bigger vision than mere money-making. Making a difference in the world enhances personal success.

Obviously everyone wants to be successful, but I want to be looked back on as being very innovative, very trusted and ethical and ultimately making a big difference in the world.
Sergey Brin, co-founder and president of Google Inc.

Aspire to decency. Practice civility toward one another. Admire and emulate ethical behavior wherever you find it. Apply a rigid standard of morality to your lives; and if, periodically, you fail—as you surely will—adjust your lives, not the standards.
Ted Koppel, journalist and former news anchor

Never suppose that in any possible situation or under any circumstances that it is best for you to do a dishonorable thing however slightly so it may appear to you ... Encourage all your virtuous dispositions, and exercise them whenever an opportunity arises, being assured that they will gain strength by exercise ... and that exercise will make them habitual ...
Thomas Jefferson, US president 1801–1809

I'm convinced that we can write and live our own scripts more than most people will acknowledge. I also know the price that must be paid. It's a real struggle to do it. It requires visualization and affirmation. It involves living a life of integrity, starting with making and keeping promises, until the whole human personality, the senses, the thinking, the feeling, and the intuition, are ultimately integrated and harmonized.
Stephen Covey, management consultant

During the century just passed, we humans learned how to transplant hearts, fly spaceships, clone sheep and squeeze a library's worth of data into a single slender disk. But as world events reflect, we remain far from mastering the art of human relations. We have invented no technology that will guide us to the destinations that matter most. After two world wars, the Holocaust, multiple genocides and countless conflicts, we must ask how long it will be before we are able to rise above the national, racial and gender distinctions that divide us and embrace the common humanity that binds us. The answer depends not on the stars or some mysterious forces of history; it depends on the choices that you and I and all of us make.

Madeleine Albright, former US secretary of state

Promote the well-being of others

Your well-being and that of others are intertwined.

Consider the following. We humans are social beings. We come into the world as the result of others' actions. We survive here in dependence on others. Whether we like it or not, there is hardly a moment of our lives when we do not benefit from others' activities. For this reason, it is hardly surprising that most of our happiness arises in the context of our relationships with others ... Sickness, old age, mishaps of one sort or another are the same for us all. But the sufferings which undermine our internal peace—anxiety, doubt, disappointment— these things are definitely less. In our concern for others, we worry less about ourselves. When we worry less about ourselves an experience of our own suffering is less intense.

What does this tell us? Firstly, because our every action has a universal dimension, a potential impact on others' happiness, ethics are necessary as a means to ensure that we do not harm others. Secondly, it tells us that genuine happiness consists in those spiritual qualities of love, compassion, patience, tolerance, and forgiveness and so on. For it is these which provide both for our happiness and others' happiness.

Tenzin Gyatso, The Dalai Lama

As you continue to make the choices that define your life ... you also will be defining the world you live in. Think of it as your personal version of what in the scientific world (or perhaps the science fiction world) is known as the butterfly effect. The butterfly effect holds that the smallest of actions— say, the flapping of the wings of a butterfly in the mountains of Bolivia—can lead over time to enormous consequences— say, a hurricane in Africa.

Arthur Sulzberger, Jr., publisher of The New York Times

Sometimes even more demanding than the physical courage to face danger is the moral courage to do what's right: doing your job the way it's supposed to be done, even if others advocate the easy way; choosing the harder right over the easier wrong, even if you have to take a hit for speaking up for what you think is true.

Paul Wolfowitz, president of the World Bank

I shall do less whenever I shall believe what I am doing hurts the cause and I shall do more whenever I shall believe doing more will help the cause. I shall try to correct errors when shown to be errors and I shall adopt new views so fast as they shall appear to be true views.

Abraham Lincoln, US president 1861–1865

I could urge you all to work hard, save, and prosper. And I do. But transcending all else is being principled in how you go about doing those things. It is decidedly not true that "nice guys finish last," as that highly original American baseball philosopher Leo Durocher was once alleged to have said.

Alan Greenspan, five-times chairman of the US Federal Reserve

Treat others as you want to be treated

It's the golden rule: "Do unto others as you would have them do unto you." Imagine yourself in another person's place.

Well, see, if you adhere to some kind of moral code, whatever it is, it makes it a more efficient way to deal with people. One time I got caught being catty about someone and got busted for it. I realized that it made my position with that person and with the people who were witness to it weaker. So I decided that you have a contract with someone and if you're trying to break that contract, your case is weaker if you haven't lived up to all your parts. And every single day, we have little social contracts and the strengthening of my will just made it easier to deal with situations head on.

Linda Ronstadt, singer

I hope you will always fight for the right of others to speak out, even if you don't like them or their views. We must protect the right to seem stupid, to seem foolish, to seem wrong. Because the truth will finally emerge, not from the mouth of one great leader, but from the conflicting opinions and honest debate of people like you.

Eric Schlosser, writer and activist

You know how, when you're a kid and somebody is making fun of the fat kid on the bus, this little voice inside you says, "This is not right"? Well, that little voice stays there, and you spend your whole life trying to shorten the gap between that internal voice and what you actually say. Sometimes you don't even understand the ramifications, but you just can't live with yourself if you don't say something.

Susan Sarandon, actor

This world truly does require your help. It requires your ears. It requires your pausing a moment before you get flippant with somebody ... You've got to pause. The world right now is about pause—before you speak, before you pass judgment, before you decide what somebody else is not, check your own basket. Check your own basket. If you hear nothing else today, if you take nothing else with you, before you go to make that judgment, check your own basket. Because what you say, and how you act towards people, has taken on new meaning.

Whoopi Goldberg, actor

Remember that those who do good, do well

In the long run, excellence can only be achieved honorably.

One law that surprised some people is the spiritual principle that those who do good, do well. Millions of people think that in order to get ahead, you have to be selfish. Actually, people who achieved success were those who tried to help others. Take this simple example. There are two stores—one run by a selfish manager, and the other run by a manager who tries to help his employees and the public and to give better value. The one that tries to help other people gets more customers and better employees, and forges ahead. The other usually fails.

Sir John Templeton, *investor; founder of The Templeton Foundation*

I do not deny that many appear to have succeeded in a material way by cutting corners and manipulating associates, both in their professional and in their personal lives. But material success is possible in this world, and far more satisfying, when it comes without exploiting others. The true measure of a career is to be able to be content, even proud, that you succeeded through your own endeavors without leaving a trail of casualties in your wake.

Alan Greenspan, *five-times chairman of the US Federal Reserve*

BEING
FLEXIBLE

One of the most important ingredients of excellence is the ability to be flexible, to adapt to and even embrace inevitable changes. It's the ability to be self-critical and to self-correct. You may have a focus and a goal, but to be successful it's a good idea to be open to feedback from the outside. In an increasingly complex world, it helps to be willing to evaluate yourself, and, when necessary, to change.

The things we fear most in organizations—fluctuations, disturbances, imbalances—are the primary sources of creativity.
Margaret Wheatley, management consultant

Prepare yourself for the world, as the athletes used to do for their exercise; oil your mind and your manners, to give them the necessary suppleness and flexibility; strength alone will not do.
Philip Stanhope, 4th Earl of Chesterfield, British statesman

The bend in the road is not the end of the road unless you refuse to take the turn.
Anonymous

Invite surprise

Plan your path to excellence, but leave room for the twists and turns. Live your life as if you were plotting a thriller.

... Expect surprise. In fact, invite surprise. Each time you begin some next chapter, your composition of yourself will be at risk. But that's OK—that's good—because you will not live fully if you never displace yourself ... E. L. Doctorow once said, "You may be able to see only as far as your headlights, but you can make the whole trip that way."
Wally Lamb, writer

New ideas stir from every corner. They show up disguised innocently as interruptions, contradictions and embarrassing dilemmas. Beware of total strangers and friends alike who shower you with comfortable sameness, and remain open to those who make you uneasy, for they are the true messengers of the future.
Rob Lebow, corporate consultant

Do something spontaneous.

Everything I do comes spontaneous. Sometimes it takes a long time; sometimes it comes just like that.
Ravi Shankar, musician

I created *The Simpsons* on the spot, thinking that if it did fail, I could just go back and draw rabbits, and no-one would be the wiser.
Matt Groening, cartoonist

Being open to change is not a passive act. You need to deliberately expose yourself to chance.

Contrary to what you might think—"preparing for the unexpected" involves a little bit more than being radically open to whatever the universe sends your way, while you lean back into the lawnchair of life. To truly prepare for the unexpected, you've got to position yourself to keep a couple of options open—so when the door of opportunity opens, you're close enough to squeeze through.

Pierre Omidyar, founder of eBay

Because of the routines we follow, we often forget that life is an ongoing adventure. We leave our homes for work, acting and even believing that we will reach our destinations with no unusual event startling us out of our set expectations. The truth is we know nothing, not where our cars will fail or when our buses will stall, whether our places of employment will be there when we arrive, or whether, in fact, we ourselves will arrive whole and alive at the end of our journeys. Life is pure adventure and the sooner we realize that, the quicker we will be able to treat life as art: to bring all our energies to each encounter, to remain flexible enough to notice and admit when what we expected to happen did not happen. We need to remember that we are created creative and can invent new scenarios as frequently as they are needed.

Maya Angelou, writer and poet

Test your own convictions

One of the most difficult things many successful people do is to challenge their own beliefs. Convictions that may have once been true and useful may change. Will you?

Friedrich Nietzsche said it well when he said, "It's not simply a question of having the courage of one's convictions, but at times having the courage to attack one's convictions." That's how you grow. That how you mature. That's how you develop. Look at Malcolm X himself, what a great example of a man who was willing to grow because he realized that he had to attack, at times, his own convictions. Socrates said it well when he said, "The unexamined life is not worth living." But we need to add that the examined life is painful, risky, full of vulnerability. And, yet, to revitalize public conversation, we have to ensure that self-criticism and self-correction are accented both in our individual lives, as well as in our society and world.

Cornel West, scholar and philosopher

… When faced with the inevitable, you always have a choice. You may not be able to alter reality, but you can alter your attitude towards it. As I learned during my liberal arts education, any symbol can have, in the imaginative context, two versions, a positive and a negative. Blood can either be the gift of life or what comes out of you when you cut your wrists in the bathtub. Or, somewhat less drastically, if you spill your milk you're left with a glass which is either half empty or half full.

Margaret Atwood, writer

... There are two ways you encounter things in the world that are different. One is everything that comes in reinforces what you already believe and everything that you know. The other thing is that you stay flexible enough or curious enough and maybe unsure of yourself enough, or may be you are more sure of yourself—I don't know which it is—that the new things that come in keep reforming your world view.

Jane Jacobs, writer and activist

Testing your worldview will help strengthen it and give it credibility. This method is not only true for scientists, but can also be applied to many areas of life.

Details that could throw doubt on your interpretation must be given, if you know them. You must do the best you can— if you know anything at all wrong, or possibly wrong— to explain it. If you make a theory, for example, and advertise it, or put it out, then you must also put down all the facts that disagree with it, as well as those that agree with it. There is also a more subtle problem. When you have put a lot of ideas together to make an elaborate theory, you want to make sure, when explaining what it fits, that those things it fits are not just the things that gave you the idea for the theory; but that the finished theory makes something else come out right, in addition.

In summary, the idea is to give all of the information to help others to judge the value of your contribution; not just the information that leads to judgment in one particular direction or another.

Richard Feynman, Nobel Laureate in Physics

Evolve and adapt

The world is always changing. Be conscious of these changes. Compromise when appropriate. The more successful you are, the more conscious and adaptable you must be.

I'm a catalyst for change ... You can't be an outsider and be successful over 30 years without leaving a certain amount of scar tissue around the place.
Rupert Murdoch, *chairman and managing director of News Corporation*

Change your language and you change your thoughts.
Karl Albrecht, *management consultant*

... If you look at my career, I always try to break my own image. My big fight has always been: Don't put me into a mold, 'cause I'm not going to go into it. Just when you think you can imitate me when my hair's long, I cut it short; when you think my hair's brown, I make it red; when they imitate me with long nails, I cut 'em off. I don't want that kind of success. I want to grow as an artist. As a human being. I'm not interested in images or in being imitated.
Barbra Streisand, *singer and actor*

When people say things like, Bill Gates controls this or Malone controls this or Ovitz controls that, I hope people don't really believe it. Because every day we're saying: How can we keep this customer happy? How can we get ahead in innovation by doing this, because if we don't, somebody else will? If anything, people underestimate how effective capitalism is at keeping even the most successful companies on the edge.
Bill Gates, *founder of Microsoft*

I used to think that compromise in life, as in art, was unthinkable, that the worst thing a man could do was make compromises. But of course I did make compromises. We all do. We have to. We couldn't live otherwise. But for a long time I wouldn't admit to myself—although, of course, at the same time I knew it—that I, too, was a man who compromised. I thought I could be above it all. I have learned that I can't. I have learned that what matters, really, is being alive. You're alive; you can't stand dead or half-dead people, can you? To me, what counts is being able to feel.

Ingmar Bergman, film director

BEING HUMBLE

*Excellence is characterized by a quiet
confidence. It's sureness without cockiness.
It's an honorable humbleness. It's a state
of mind that transcends petty differences.
It liberates you from the desire for constant
acknowledgment. You don't need to brag or
boast. You drop any feelings of entitlement.
You recognize greatness in others as well as
in yourself. A person of excellence doesn't
expect or demand great things to happen.
They just do.*

It is always the secure who are humble.
G. K. Chesterton, writer

No. 1, we have got to remain humble, we have got to remember our roots. Too many companies forget their beginnings and that is where it all goes wrong.
Tony Fernandes, CEO of AirAsia

A man wrapped up in himself makes a very small bundle.
Benjamin Franklin, founding father of the United States

Fight your ego

Remember that you are part of – and depend upon – the rest of the world. This will help you maintain a respect for others and to cultivate their well-being just as you cultivate yours.

Real excellence and humility are not incompatible one with the other, on the contrary they are twin sisters.
Jean Baptiste Lacordaire, orator

It is well to remember that the entire population of the universe, with one trifling exception, is composed of others.
Andrew J. Holmes, writer

Sure I am a religious man who is also passionate about conserving the environment. But I am also a CEO, with all the bad habits and attitudes that are natural to the species ... I am still naturally self-interested, overconfident, full of pride, and eager to control a meeting as any CEO in America. Every day, I struggle with my ego.
Tom Chappell, founder of Tom's of Maine

Humiliation. Always remember, my good friends, that there is one sin we must never commit and it is to humiliate another person or to allow another person to be humiliated in our presence without us screaming and shouting and protesting. Learn that. Poverty is humiliation. There is absolutely no reason in the world why some people should be poor when we are not. Exclusion, discrimination, is humiliation. There is absolutely no reason in the world why I should be happier than anyone else, in my place, in my home, and in my work.
Elie Wiesel, writer and Holocaust survivor, and Nobel Peace Prize Laureate

… We must divest ourselves of our egotistical anthropocentrism, our habit of seeing ourselves as masters of the universe who can do whatever occurs to us. We must discover a new respect for what transcends us: for the universe, for the earth, for nature, for life, and for reality. Our respect for other people, for other nations and for other cultures, can only grow from a humble respect for the cosmic order and from an awareness that we are a part of it, that we share in it and that nothing of what we do is lost, but rather becomes part of the eternal memory of being, where it is judged.

Vaclav Havel, playwright and former president of the Czech Republic

Glory is largely a theatrical concept. There is no striving for glory without a vivid awareness of an audience.

Eric Hoffer, writer and activist

Not all glory is self-glory. It is far more impressive when others discover your good qualities without your help.

When I was a young man, I thought glory was the highest attainment, and all glory was self-glory. My parents tried to teach me otherwise, as did my church, as did the Naval Academy. But I didn't understand the lesson until later in life, when I confronted challenges I never expected to face. In that confrontation, I discovered that I was dependent on others to a greater extent than I had ever realized, but neither they nor the cause we served made any claims on my identity. On the contrary, they gave me a larger sense of myself than I had before. And I am a better man for it. I discovered that nothing in life is more liberating than to fight for a cause that encompasses you but is not defined by your existence alone. And that has made all the difference, my friends, all the difference in the world.

John McCain, US senator

Being humble also relieves the stress that accompanies the belief that you're at the center of the universe.

The first step to becoming a more peaceful person is to have the humility to admit that, in most cases, you're creating your own emergencies. Life will usually go on if things don't go according to plan. It's helpful to keep reminding yourself and repeating the sentence, "Life isn't an emergency".

Richard Carlson, writer

Never presume

Don't assume that the world will revolve around you, or even that a past success will endure. Once you lapse into a state of expectation, you're bound to be disappointed.

... In my own little country, in my own foreign ministry, I spend a lot of time trying again and again to improve our internal performance, even in details like punctuality, in terms of the way we deliver services to our people, in the way we examine promotions to ensure they are fair, the way I insist again and again that more women should be brought into the ministry at senior leadership levels. If I don't do that and I think only of the grander, exterior aspects of my ministry, like opening more embassies, having more diplomatic activities, well, I don't have a solid house, a foundation behind me to sustain it. It could collapse.

José Ramos-Horta, prime minister of East Timor and Nobel Peace Prize Laureate

The other day I was hunting for mushrooms. I thought there might be mushrooms around because it had rained a little bit, then it got sunny, and then it rained again. I looked around very casually. I saw a beautiful patch, and I got all excited. I found quite a few mushrooms, gathered them up in my shirt, and took them back to the kitchen. I bragged and said, "Look at all these chanterelles I found." Then, today ... I thought, "I know I can find lots of them." Once I had that expectation, I couldn't find a single one. But when the expectation waned, sure enough, there they were.

Willem Dafoe, *actor*

Class is an aura of confidence that is being sure without being cocky. Class has nothing to do with money. Class never runs scared. It is self-discipline and self-knowledge. It's the sure footedness that comes with having proved you can meet life.

Ann Landers, *advice columnist*

Don't fall for flattery

Flattery is all right so long as you don't inhale.

Adlai Stevenson, *American politician; presidential candidate in 1952 and 1956*

Barbara Corday, the CBS executive, came over and said, "You're a genius! There's Robin Williams and there's you. You're lightning in a bottle." A week later, they fired all the other actors and rewrote the script and fired the director. Corday told me, "We want to bring an acting teacher in for you." I said, "Does that mean I'm no longer lightning in a bottle?" Had I believed the first remark, the second one would have devastated me. But I knew better.

George Clooney, *actor*

BEING INCISIVE

A sign of excellence is the ability to think and act with clarity. The incisive person is clear in his or her head. Although absolute certainty is impossible, it's important to be incisive enough to take action based on the information on hand. Deliberate, but don't be afraid to act. And once you do make a decision, you must be able to make the best of it.

The simplest answer is to act.
Fortune cookie

The way to get started is to quit talking and begin doing.
Walt Disney

The hardest thing to learn in life is which bridge to cross and which to burn.
David Russell, musician

Act as if you're sure even when you're not

You're faced with decisions every day. Make an informed choice and act with confidence.

Next in importance to having a good aim is to recognize when to pull the trigger.
David Letterman, talk show host

You have to pretend you're 100 per cent sure. You have to take action; you can't hesitate or hedge your bets. Anything less will condemn your efforts to failure.
Andrew Grove, founder of Intel Corp.

… You will have to rely upon an inner compass; for only you can set the standards by which your life will be measured. Each day, you will face decisions in which your sense of purpose will compete against temptations, distractions and confusions. You will often be uncertain, for the path to a life of fulfillment and accomplishment is nowhere clearly marked.
Madeleine Albright, former US secretary of state

Never again clutter your days or nights with so many menial and unimportant things that you have no time to accept a real challenge when it comes along. This applies to play as well as work. A day merely survived is no cause for celebration.
You are not here to fritter away your precious hours when you have the ability to accomplish so much by making a slight change in your routine. No more busy work. No more hiding from success. Leave time, leave space, to grow. Now. Now! Not tomorrow!
Og Mandino, author of The Greatest Salesman in the World

Remember it's also a decision not to act.

What you have to do is make a decision. Life is very rarely a 90-10 decision. Most of the decisions I make are inside the 45-yard lines, they're not easy. There's a case on both sides. But you make the decision. The only decision that is absolutely unfixable is if you don't make a decision. Because that is a decision; not to act. And that decision, almost always, leads to some kind of failure. So you obviously try to maximize the time you have to make the decision, you make it, and as soon as you know it's a bad one make another one. The most important thing is to continue to make decisions.
Roger Ailes, *chairman, CEO and president of Fox News*

You do things when the opportunities come along. I've had periods in my life when I've had a bundle of ideas come along, and I've had long dry spells. If I get an idea next week, I'll do something. If not, I won't do a damn thing.
Warren Buffett, *investor; chairman of Berkshire Hathaway*

Don't waste (too much) time agonizing

A good solution applied with vigor now is better than a perfect solution applied ten minutes later.
George S. Patton, Jr., *US general*

In the words of the ancients, one should make his decisions within the space of seven breaths. Lord Takanobu said, "If discrimination is long, it will spoil." Lord Naoshige said, "When matters are done leisurely, seven out of ten will turn out badly. A warrior is a person who does things quickly." When your mind is going hither and thither, discrimination will never be brought to a conclusion. With an intense, fresh and un-delaying spirit, one will make his judgments within the space of seven breaths. It is a matter of being determined and having the spirit to break right through to the other side.
Yamamoto Tsunetomo, *samurai, Hagakure*

If you don't act now while it's fresh in your mind, it will probably join the list of things you were always going to do but never quite got around to. Chances are you'll also miss some opportunities.

Paul Clitheroe, *motivational speaker*

Faced with excruciating decisions daily, judges are perhaps in the best position to offer advice.

The best advice I received ... was from a former law school dean, Bayless Manning. And I shall repeat it. Bayless understood that I, like you, was anxiously wondering: What comes next? He pointed out that, when we make an important personal decision, we rarely know more than ten per cent of all we would like to know. We know that our decision will open certain doors, but we often cannot know which ones it will close. We agonize over the decision, but sometimes agonizing does not help. Sometimes we must simply choose. Once we reach a decision, our lives then shape themselves around the choices that we make.

Stephen Breyer, *associate justice, US Supreme Court*

For all of life's disparities in talent and wealth, each of us is given exactly the same amount of time in each hour, and in each day, and in each year. It is a limited amount, and it is impossible for anyone to be so rich in "time" that he can enjoy every single one of the things which time may buy. So, as I have said earlier, there are choices to be made. But it is very important for each of us that these choices be made consciously, with as much knowledge as possible of their consequences. You should consider these choices not only in terms of financial reward, and enjoyment of work, but in

terms of how much time they will demand. The Greek
philosopher Theophrastus said more than 2,000 years ago
that "Time is the most valuable thing a man can spend."
The French satirist Rabelais said pretty much the same thing
1800 years later: "Nothing is so dear and precious as time."
William Rehnquist, *former chief justice, US Supreme Court*

Compartmentalize

*The ability to break down a problem into separate
steps, or to separate action from emotion may help you
be more incisive.*

… I think I'm really good at compartmentalizing. I'm more
lucid about my own work if I have got something to distract
me. I can be making a movie and then I can go off that movie
for a half an hour while they are lighting the set and I can be
looking at the script and making changes with the writer on my
next movie. I come back to the film I'm working on with a great
deal of objectivity. Subjectivity is the director's worst enemy.
Steven Spielberg, *film director; three-times Academy Award winner*

I learned that we can do anything, but we can't do everything
… at least not at the same time. So think of your priorities not
in terms of what activities you do, but when you do them.
Timing is everything.
Dan Millman, *motivational writer*

BEING
INTUITIVE

Some of the world's most successful people credit their intuition as their most important trait. Intuition comprises gut instincts, first impressions, an inner voice. Strong intuition will help you avoid pitfalls. It will help you to know when to question and when to trust; when to stop and when to go. Being intuitive requires self-confidence. Have faith in your inner voice when it speaks to you.

We easily ignore our instincts, even when they're yelling at us.
Billie G. Blair, organizational psychologist

I feel there are two people inside me—me and my intuition.
If I go against her, she'll screw me every time, and if I follow
her, we get along quite nicely.
Kim Basinger, actor

Trust the inner voice

Intuition is the small voice inside you that tells you exactly what to think.

You have to leave the city of your comfort and go into the wilderness of your intuition. What you'll discover will be wonderful. What you'll discover is yourself.
Alan Alda, actor

Intuition is a combination of historical (empirical) data, deep and heightened observation, and an ability to cut through the thickness of surface reality. Intuition is like a slow motion machine that captures data instantaneously and hits you like a ton of bricks. Intuition is a knowing, a sensing that is beyond the conscious understanding—a gut feeling. Intuition is not pseudo-science.
Abella Arthur, career coach

I followed no system. I worked intuitively. My aim every time was do a book, to create something that would be easy and interesting to read. At every stage I could only work within my knowledge and sensibility and talent and world-view.
Sir Vidiadhar Surajprasad (V.S.) Naipaul, writer and
Nobel Laureate in Literature

Trust your hunches. They're usually based on facts filed away just below the conscious level.
Joyce Brothers, psychologist and advice columnist

There can be as much value in the blink of an eye as in months of rational analysis.
Malcolm Gladwell, writer

Man is born a potentially complete success. The reason humanity loves its children is that they start off in such perfection of potential. Man, as designed, is obviously intended to be a success just as the hydrogen atom is intended to be a success. It is only [because of] the fabulous ignorance of man and his long and wrongly conditioned reflexes that he continually allowed the new life to be impaired albeit lovingly and unwittingly.

R. Buckminster Fuller, *visionary, designer, and inventor*

Your inner voice might be the voice of reason.

Next time somebody tells you something that sounds important, think to yourself, "Is this the kind of thing that people probably know because of evidence or is it the kind of thing that people only believe because of tradition, authority or revelation?" And next time somebody tells you that something is true, why not say to them, "What kind of evidence is there for that?" And if they can't give you a good answer, I hope you'll think very carefully before you believe a word they say.

Richard Dawkins, *evolutionary biologist*

Follow your own instincts

Sometimes your instincts might be irrational or counterintuitive. But it's better to follow your own instincts than someone else's.

Once I began following my own instincts, sales took off and I became a millionaire. And that, I think, is a key secret to every person's success, be they male or female, banker or pornographer: Trust in your gut.

Larry Flynt, publisher

I don't think that we can allow other people's perceptions to be the thing that either puts us onto a course that's unnatural for us or persuades us to pursue something that doesn't come out of our own gut. The truth is we'll do the best that we can, and I guess that there are some people who will be excited and enthusiastic, and there will be some who will be skeptical and disappointed. You can't be guided by other people's expectations.

Jeffrey Katzenberg, co-founder, Dream Works SKG

Sometimes you need to remove yourself from the noise to hear your inner voice.

Listen once in a while. It's amazing what you can hear. On a hot summer day in the country you can hear the corn growing, the crack of a tin roof buckling under the power of the sun. In a real old-fashioned parlor silence so deep you can hear the dust settling on the velveteen settee, you might hear the footsteps of something sinister gaining on you, or a heart-stoppingly beautiful phrase from Mozart you haven't heard since childhood, or the voice of somebody—now gone—whom you loved. Or sometime when you're talking up a storm so brilliant, so charming that you can hardly believe how wonderful you are, pause just a moment and listen to yourself. It's good for the soul to hear yourself as others hear you, and next time maybe, just maybe, you will not talk so much, so loudly, so brilliantly, so charmingly, so utterly shamefully foolishly.

Russell Baker, *writer and Pulitzer Prize winner*

BEING LIKED AND LOVED

An excellent life is balanced between career success and the emotional fulfillment you get from friends and loved ones. The latter infuses life with meaning and purpose. The people you trust give you feedback and direction. They keep you in touch with your values. They remind you of your dreams. They enhance your life in infinite ways. They remind you why the pursuit of excellence is worthwhile—and achievable.

I believe that being successful means having a balance of success stories across the many areas of your life. You can't truly be considered successful in your business life if your home life is in shambles.
Zig Ziglar, motivational speaker

One must be fond of people and trust them if one is not to make a mess of life.
E. M. Forster, writer

To live without loving is to not really live.
Molière (Jean-Baptiste Poquelin), playwright, director, and actor

Find people to trust

At various points in your life you'll need someone to provide insights. Have on tap a person whose opinion you trust.

It's very important to have someone whom you trust who can bring in another perspective. When Bernie Taupin and I started out we were trying to write songs for other people. Then a guy called Steve Brown came along and said, "You've got to go on the road. You've got to get a band. You've got to start doing this yourself." I had no aspirations at that point to be an artist. But Steve saw it in me, and he nurtured me. He was my right-hand man. Muff Winwood, Steve Winwood's brother, is someone else who was a really big help to me in the beginning … Muff would tell me the truth, and that was very important. It's crucial for an artist to have an ear like that. You have to have someone who a) believes in you, b) will tell you the truth, and c) will be there for you when you phone at 2am in the midst of a crisis.

Elton John, singer, songwriter and musician

… Cherish your human connections: your relationships with family and friends … As important as your obligations as a doctor, a lawyer, a business leader will be, you are a human being first. And those human connections—with spouses, with children, with friends—are the most important investments you will ever make.

At the end of your life, you will never regret not having passed one more test, winning one more verdict, or not closing one more deal. You will regret time not spent with a husband, a child, a friend, or a parent.

Barbara Bush, former US first lady

Have a loving companion

Some claim that nothing is more important to excellence than finding a loving mate, companion, or spouse.

Find a loving mate to share what life has in store, because the world can be a lonely place, and people who aren't lonely don't want to hear about it if you are. At some point you're going to tire of yourself, of the sound of your own voice (if you haven't already), and you're going to need someone whose voice you never tire of, someone who'll know you better, in some ways, than you know yourself and who'll remind you who you are when you forget and why things matter. After 30 years, my wife Barbara and I continue to delight in each other's company, and that's astonishing given the number of other people we've grown weary of. I have to tell you that the odds of finding the right person to spend an entire life with are not great, and if you get it wrong, badly wrong, your good life will morph in abject misery.
Richard Russo, *writer*

Love one person, take care of them until you die. You know, raise kids. Have a good life. Be a good friend. And try to be completely who you are. And figure out what you personally love. And like go after it with everything you've got no matter how much it takes.
Angelina Jolie, *actor*

Make friends

The friends you make just might help your career as well.

I took a boat to England to pursue graduate studies at Oxford, because I loved history and philosophy ... The beginning of that trip was not particularly auspicious. A few days at sea and my intestines told me I had committed a grave error. I retreated to my tiny cabin where I thought I would die. Then came a knock at the door, and I opened it to find a tall, gangly young man about my age who spoke in a smooth southern accent. He held chicken soup in one hand and crackers in the other, and he said, "Hi, I'm Bill Clinton, and I heard you weren't feeling well so I thought maybe these would help." One thing he did not say was: I feel your pain. That came later. Twenty-five years later he asked me to be in his cabinet.

Robert Reich, *former US secretary of labor*

You can make more friends in two months by becoming interested in other people than you can in two years by trying to get other people interested in you.

Dale Carnegie, *author of* How to Win Friends and Influence People

Be there for others

Your personal life will inform and enrich your professional life, if you let it.

A few years ago my colleague Russell Baker, the distinguished *New York Times* columnist and humorist was asked by the *Times* in-house magazine to write a piece about a colleague who had just been promoted to a powerful new position. Baker went to see his own great mentor James Reston, then the *Times* bureau chief. He mentioned the colleague's name to Reston. "Tell me about his life," Baker asked Reston. "That's not a life—that's a career," Reston said with great disdain. He meant that the colleague had at once done everything right, but had somehow missed the point of what he had done; he had covered the requisite big stories, had made the front page the requisite number of times, but he had in some way failed in the elemental human involvement so necessary for real pleasure in this career. He won all the prizes save the real ones, the friendships and all the fun that are at the core of what we do.

David Halberstam, *historian and journalist*

Love is the expression of one's values, the greatest reward you can earn for the moral qualities you have achieved in your character and person, the emotional price paid by one man for the joy he receives from the virtues of another.

Ayn Rand, *writer and philosopher*

BEING MEANINGFUL

An excellent life is full of meaning and purpose. Meaningfulness is different from mere success. It means asking: Am I fulfilled?

At the end of the day, are you usually energized or depleted? Would you want to continue what you're doing for the next 30 years? In what ways would you supplement your life? What legacy do you want to leave?

Hold onto your dreams. Take up the challenge of forging an identity that transcends yourself. Transcend yourself and you will find yourself. Care about something you needn't bother with at all. Throw yourself into the world and make your voice count.

Hillary Clinton, US senator

So many people walk around with a meaningless life. They seem half-asleep, even when they're busy doing things they think are important. This is because they're chasing the wrong things. The way you get meaning into your life is to devote yourself to loving others, devote yourself to your community around you, and devote yourself to creating something that gives you purpose and meaning.

Morrie Schwartz, educator

The meaning of things lies not in the things themselves, but in our attitude towards them.

Antoine de Saint-Exupéry, writer

Embrace a cause

Excellence is not simply self-mastery, but mastery of a cause. Find strength in the fact that you're not alone and that your actions contribute to a cause, whether in politics, business, or in other spheres of life.

Many years ago I read in the writings of George Bernard Shaw a passage that moved me and found an answering echo in my mind and heart. He wrote: "This is the true joy in life, the being used for a purpose recognized by yourself as a mighty one; the being thoroughly worn out before you are thrown on the scrap heap; the being a force of Nature instead of a feverish, selfish little clod of ailments and grievances, complaining that the world will not devote itself to making you happy." The only ambition I have is that, to the end of my days, I should work my hardest, and then, when I have done my job, that I should be thrown on the scrap heap. When I have done my job, there is no need to bother about me further.
Jawaharlal Nehru, prime minister of India 1947–1964

I am here to be a citizen in a pluralist democracy. I am here to be effective, to have agency, to make a claim on power, to spread it around, to rearrange it, to democratize it, to legislate it into justice. Why you? Because the world will end if you don't act. You are the citizen of a flawed but actual democracy. Citizens are not actually capable of not acting, it is not given to a citizen that she doesn't act, this is the price you pay for being a citizen of a democracy, your life is married to the political beyond the possibility of divorcement. You are always an agent. When you don't act, you act. When you don't vote, you vote. When you accept the loony logic of some of the left that there is no political value in supporting the lesser of two evils, you open the door to the greater evil.
Tony Kushner, playwright

Find something that moves you or pisses you off, and do something about it. Put your self out there. Be brave. Be bold. Take action. You have a voice. Speak up, especially when something tries to keep you silent. Take a stand for what's right. Raise a ruckus and make a change. You may not always be popular, but you'll be part of something larger and bigger and greater than yourself. Besides, making history is extremely cool.

Samuel L. Jackson, *actor*

By expanding your focus beyond yourself, you will enhance your meaningfulness.

Focusing your life solely on making a buck shows a poverty of ambition. It asks too little of yourself. You need to take up the challenges that we face as a nation and make them your own, not because you have an obligation to those who are less fortunate, although you do have that obligation. Not because you have a debt to all of those who helped you get to where you are, although you do have that debt ... You need to take on the challenge because you have an obligation to yourself. Because our individual salvation depends on collective salvation. Because it's only when you hitch your wagon to something larger than yourself that you will realize your true potential.

Barack Obama, *US senator*

Help publicly. Help privately. Help in your actions by recycling and conserving and protecting, but help also in your attitude. Help make sense where sense has gone missing. Help bring reason and respect to discourse and debate. Help science to solve and faith to soothe. Help law bring justice, until justice is commonplace. Help and you will abolish apathy—the void that is so quickly filled by ignorance and evil.

Tom Hanks, *actor*

My hope is that whatever you do to make a good life for yourself—whether you become a teacher, or social worker, or business person, or lawyer, or poet, or scientist—you will devote part of your life to making this a better world for your children, for all children. My hope is that your generation will demand an end to war, that your generation will do something that has not yet been done in history and wipe out the national boundaries that separate us from other human beings on this earth.

Howard Zinn, historian and political scientist

Believe in something and fight for those beliefs.

Always, always, do the things that you believe. Don't become monuments—sway with the wind. Change opinions, if the change is natural and believed. But believe in something and fight for those beliefs. Honor them by your commitment. Further them by your effort.

And what a wondrous and what an incredibly grand world you might build for your children. Now this millennium may not be in sight, let alone in reach. The route to it may be pretty damned close to impassable. It may be as distant and as complicated to reach as the moon or another solar system. BUT IT IS THERE! It's there for the taking, the asking and the fighting.

Rod Serling, screenwriter, 1950s and 1960s

Step outside your own existence.

It is the business of the future to be dangerous, and most of the people who magnify its risks do so for reasons of their own. Jealous of a future apt to render them ridiculous or irrelevant, they bear comparison to the French noblewoman, a duchess in her eighties, who, on seeing the first ascent of Montgolfier's balloon from the palace of the Tuileries in 1783, fell back upon the cushions of her carriage and wept. "Oh yes," she said, "now it's certain. One day they'll learn how to keep people alive for ever, but I shall already be dead."
Louis Lapham, editor and journalist

Empowered by a meaningful cause, you may find that it's easier to stand up against adversity.

When we were screening the film *Arth* for possible distributors, everyone said it was a wonderful film but it would not run a day unless we changed the end because an Indian woman rejecting her husband after he has apologized is completely unacceptable. Mahesh Bhatt and I dug our heels in and said that this was precisely why we were making this film and we were going to stick with the ending. It came as a huge surprise to us that the film became a very big success. Apart from winning me the National Award, it also became in a sense a cult film. Suddenly, I had women walk into my house expecting me to resolve all their marital problems. They were no longer reacting to me as fans to a star, but as a sister, as a woman. I was overwhelmed and I was really scared because I had not really given it a moment's thought and then I realized that in fact I am being put in a position of great responsibility.
Shabana Azmi, actress, activist, member of the Indian Parliament, and UN goodwill ambassador

Construct meaning from experience

A meaningful life is led consciously.

Teaching you how to think is actually shorthand for a much deeper, more serious idea: learning how to think really means learning how to exercise some control over how and what you think. It means being conscious and aware enough to choose what you pay attention to and to choose how you construct meaning from experience. Because if you cannot exercise this kind of choice in adult life, you will be totally hosed. Think of the old cliché about ... the mind being an excellent servant but a terrible master.

This, like many clichés, so lame and unexciting on the surface, actually expresses a great and terrible truth.
David Foster Wallace, writer

Perhaps it would be a good idea, fantastic as it sounds, to muffle every telephone, stop every motor, and halt all activity for an hour some day, to give people a chance to ponder for a few minutes on what it is all about, why they are living and what they really want.
James Adams, historian

To articulate what is meaningful to you, you must be prepared to be in touch with your innermost feelings. Develop an inner life and give that inner life a voice.

... To speak well we must go down as far as the bucket can be lowered. Every thought must be thought through from its ultimate cost back to its cheap beginnings; every perception, however profound and distant, must be as clear and easy as the moon; every desire must be recognized as a relative and named as fearlessly as Satan named his angels; finally, every feeling must be felt to its bottom where the bucket rests in the silt and water rises like a tower around it. To talk to ourselves well requires, then, endless rehearsals—rehearsals in which we revise, and the revision of the inner life strikes many people as hypocritical; but to think how to express some passion properly is the only way to be possessed by it, for unformed feelings lack impact, just as unfelt ideas lose weight. So walk around unrewritten, if you like. Live on broken phrases and syllable gristle, telegraphese and film reviews. No-one will suspect ... until you speak.

William Gass, writer

Infuse your work with meaning

It's not true that meaningful work is always done outside the office. Many corporate models are based on empowering employees and customers so that both the business and the individual thrive.

If the community is successful, we're successful. We make money when they're successful. That's the pure-business way of looking at it. The other way to see it ... is the concept of empowerment. EBay creates opportunities for people to do things that they could never do before: for sellers to create business, for people who work from home who don't want 9 to 5 jobs, for supplementing one's income; for buyers with specific passions to collect things by buying them on eBay; and for developers to actually create applications that make money—that's the broadest definition of empowerment. We want to teach people to fish instead of feed them.

Andre Haddad, vice president of user experience and design, eBay

... You can make money by preventing global warming and get a useful material in the process. I think there are all kinds of win-win scenarios like that out there just waiting to be discovered by adventurous souls. You just have to refuse to accept the limitations that entrenched interests would like us to believe can't be surmounted. And many people are, which makes it a lot easier for me to sleep at night.

Jeffrey Hollender, president of Seventh Generation

The creation of new scientific, technological, and medical breakthroughs is incredibly meaningful.

When I see a person who suffers from [cancer and AIDS] and dies, it takes a toll. You rationalize and say, "I'll go to my lab and work harder, and we'll discover something and make a difference." That's what happened with HIV. The death rate has fallen 90 per cent. We need to do more and these drugs won't last for ever, but there was a time when people said you couldn't even develop drugs against viruses like HIV. The same has to be done for breast cancer, ovarian cancer, leukemia, and other diseases ...

There's also an extraordinary power and dignity to many of my patients that I find bolsters me, in a paradoxical way.

Jerome Groopman, oncologist and researcher

First of all growing up in the US in the 1960s, I certainly was exposed to ideas of freedom and then in the 1970s at MIT, I worked as part of a community of programmers who co-operated and thought about the ethical and social meaning of this co-operation. When that community died in the early 80s ... the world of proprietary software, which most computer users at the time were participating in, was morally sickening. And I decided that I was going to try to create once again a community of co-operation. I realized that [all] I could get out of a life of participation in the competition to subjugate each other, which is what non-free software is, ... was money, and I would have a life that I would hate.

Richard Stallman, founder of the Free Software Foundation

Meaning creates a context for your work, which

... The best way to learn something is to try to solve real problems that are meaningful ... If, for example, you're trying to create a reading machine, then you learn about optics. And you learn about signal processing, and image enhancement techniques, and all of these different things that you need to know in order to solve the problem. If you really have a compelling need to solve these problems, you will learn about them. If you're trying to create, let's say, a hip hop song, well you learn about the history of hip hop, and how it emerged from other forms of music. And you learn something about urban culture. So learning things in context, where you're actually trying to make a contribution yourself, is a very motivating way to learn—as opposed to just trying to dryly learn facts out of context and without a purpose for learning them.

Raymond Kurzweil, artificial intelligence pioneer

Don't sell out

There's always a temptation to simply make money or climb the ladder of success. But that's not always meaningful.

Creating a life that reflects your values and satisfies your soul is a rare achievement. In a culture that relentlessly promotes avarice and excess as the good life, a person happy doing his own work is usually considered an eccentric, if not a subversive. Ambition is only understood if it's to rise to the top of some imaginary ladder of success. Someone who takes an undemanding job because it affords him the time to pursue other interests and activities is considered a flake. A person who abandons a career in order to stay home and raise children is considered not to be living up to his potential —as if a job title and salary are the sole measure of human worth. ... To invent your own life's meaning is not easy, but it's still allowed, and I think you'll be happier for the trouble.

Bill Watterson, *creator of the comic strip* Calvin and Hobbes

One of my happiest moments came, though, when I finally discovered, late in my forties, that I didn't have to accomplish something huge in order to succeed. Corollaries of this discovery were that I didn't have to save the world, publish the great American novel, or be Superwoman all the time; however, I could launch a scholarship fund for a deceased Wellesley friend, become a pretty good theater marketing director, and learn to be a more compassionate family member and friend.

Martha Mary Corinne Morrison Claiborne Boggs (aka Cokie Roberts),
journalist and author

We are at the very beginning of time for the human race. It is not unreasonable that we grapple with problems. But there are tens of thousands of years in the future. Our responsibility is to do what we can, learn what we can, improve the solutions, and pass them on.

Richard Feynman, Nobel Laureate in Physics

BEING PASSIONATE

To excel at something, you must be passionate about it. How could it be otherwise? Only passion will sustain you as you pursue your dreams. Only passion will help you rebound after a failure. Only passion will pique your curiosity. Only passion will give your work meaning. Only passion will inspire you to be extraordinary. Only passion drives excellence.

The secret of joy in work is contained in one word—
excellence. To know how to do something well is to enjoy it.
Pearl S. Buck, writer and Nobel Laureate in Literature

You've got to love what you do to really make things happen.
Philip Green, owner of BhS and Arcadia Group

There was a disturbance in my heart, a voice that spoke there
and said, "I want, I want, I want!" It happened every
afternoon, and when I tried to suppress it it got even stronger.
Saul Bellow, writer

If the mind is intensely eager, everything can be
accomplished—mountains can be crumbled into atoms.
Swami Vivikananda, Hindu mystic

Pick your passion

Anyone who has achieved excellence will attest that they picked their passion and pursued it. Honor your desires and talents.

What blows my mind is, most people say they don't know what they're passionate about.
Mike Marriner, writer

Everybody has talent, it's just a matter of moving around until you've discovered what it is. A talent is a combination of something you love a great deal, something you can lose yourself in—something that you can start at 9 in the morning, look up from your work and it's 10 o'clock at night—and something that you have a natural ability to do very well. And usually those two things go together.
George Lucas, film producer and director

I am only certain of one thing in my life. I knew what I loved to do, and I did what I loved to do. And at this point in my life I'm still loving what I do. I never did it to make a lot of money. I did it to make a living. And in doing so, I made a life. I guess what I'm saying here is that my job became my friend, my fortune and my great love. And that no matter what lofty personal goals I set for myself, life came along and whacked me upside the head and sent me in directions I never intended to go. But I learned to adjust.
Billy Joel, singer, songwriter and musician

I think the most important thing and the thing that I have thrived by is that when you listen to your own inner voice and make that the largest voice that guides you. All criticism and all nay-saying falls away ... if you can just honor your desire. To me, that is the most important thing. Honor your desire. And make that what drives you ... When you honor your desire, anything is possible. Those are my words for everybody. I think that our desires to do certain things are divinely inspired and that if we follow them out and follow them through they will take us to much better places in our lives. We can do anything.

Margaret Cho, comedian, fashion designer, and actress

Playwright Eve Ensler compares doing what she loves with her childhood passion for diving.

Love jumping higher on the bounce, love going further out, love the flipping, love the entry and the flight. Love the pain when it doesn't work out. Get back on the board. Love it 'cause it's a call in your body, 'cause it's what you need to do. Love it 'cause you can think of nothing else and you won't be satisfied 'til it's done. You don't have to wait for permission or approval. You don't have to wait for someone to pay you or even notice. You certainly don't have to wait to be rescued. This is your story. This is your adventure. This is your creation – this is your life.

Eve Ensler, playwright

Build a career on passion

How possible is it for you to pursue a career based on your deepest passion? Anyone who has achieved excellence in their career has done so because they don't perceive what they do as work. It's pleasure.

We started Yahoo in about April 1994. It started out as a way for us to keep track of things that we were interested in.
David Filo, *co-founder of Yahoo Inc.*

When I was about 20, I started writing in my diary but that certainly didn't make me think I would ever make a living out of it.
David Sedaris, *writer and humorist*

I never decided to become a writer, as people sometimes put it. I just had to write certain books, or certain poems, and then after a number of these had been written, I realized that I was a writer.
Vikram Seth, *writer*

Because the last thing, and maybe the most important thing, that I've noticed over the years of playing with people from all kinds of stylistic zones and all different types of music, and in fact the only thing that they all seem to have in common, from Sonny Rollins to Steve Reich, from David Bowie to Milton Nascimento, from Herbie Hancock to Gary Burton, is just how much fun they all have doing what they do, when they are doing it at their best.
Pat Metheny, *musician*

You've got to find what you love. And that is as true for your work as it is for your lovers. Your work is going to fill a large part of your life, and the only way to be truly satisfied is to do what you believe is great work. And the only way to do great work is to love what you do. If you haven't found it yet, keep looking. Don't settle. As with all matters of the heart, you'll know when you find it. And, like any great relationship, it just gets better and better as the years roll on. So keep looking until you find it. Don't settle.

Steve Jobs, CEO of Apple Computer

... My practical advice is that creating knowledge is what will be most exciting in life. And in order to create knowledge you have to have passion. So find a challenge that you can be passionate about, and there are many of them that are worthwhile. And if you're passionate about a worthwhile challenge, you can find the ideas to overcome that challenge.

Raymond Kurzweil, artificial intelligence pioneer

Many identify passion with youthful idealism that should be maintained at every age.

If you do not wake up every day with great passion for your work, you will be miserable. Do not just go through the motions. Never put yourself in the position of regretting what you did not try to do. Every experience, whether it is good or bad, if it is based on the passionate belief that you are doing something you love, will give you the will and the character to learn, grow and persevere. Stand up for yourself and your dreams. Do not lose your youthful idealism for the world.

George Tenet, former director of the Central Intelligence Agency

True passion is almost a spiritual experience.

Hours slide by like minutes. The accumulated clutter of day-to-day existence, the lapses of conscience, the unpaid bills, the bungled opportunities, the dust under the couch, the inescapable prison of your genes—all of it is temporarily forgotten, crowded from your thoughts by an overpowering clarity of purpose by the seriousness of the task at hand.
Jon Krakauer, mountaineer and writer

Remember money isn't everything

Many extremely successful people remind us that money isn't everything. In any case, that isn't their primary pursuit, or what sustains them.

Personally, I didn't do this to make money. When I joined the team here, when I became a musician, there was no money to be made. We were folk singers, playing in coffee houses. There was no money, and there never would be any money. The only people I knew who had ever even made a record [were] Peter, Paul and Mary, OK?

That's not why I do it. I'm happy. You know, cash is groovy. It's a great tool. I don't let it run my life. It's not why I do things, and I'm happy with that. I will, as we say in rock 'n' roll, run until the wheels come off, because I love what I do. I love creating music. I love it that I can sing. I think it's a hugely wonderful gift, and I am truly grateful for it. And I love doing it. So I'll do it until it's not fun.
David Crosby, musician

We enjoy the process far more than the proceeds.
Warren Buffett, investor; chairman of Berkshire Hathaway

I felt that I could make a difference. That's the best reason to go into business—because you feel strongly that you can change things.
Sir Richard Branson, founder of the Virgin brand

BEING PATIENT

Excellence takes time. Behind nearly every overnight success are years of hard work, dedication, and failure. Remember this in your pursuit of excellence. Remember this especially when it seems as if excellence is unattainable. Your determination and productivity must be matched with patience.

How poor are they that have not patience! What wound did ever heal but by degrees?
William Shakespeare

The pursuit of balance is a lifelong journey.
Barry Baker, president and COO, USA Networks

Genius is nothing but a great aptitude for patience.
George Louis de Buffon, naturalist

Patience and tenacity of purpose are worth more than twice their weight of cleverness.
Thomas Henry Huxley, scientist

Courage and perseverance have a magical talisman, before which difficulties disappear and obstacles vanish into air.
John Quincy Adams, US president 1825–1829

Remember that it all takes time

You will suffer if you rush; and so will your work.

It is important to have determination and optimism and patience. If you lack patience, even when you face some small obstacle, you lose courage. There is a Tibetan saying, "Even if you have failed at something nine times, you have still given it effort nine times." I think that's important. Use your brain to analyze the situation. Do not rush through it, but think. Once you decide what to do about that obstacle, then there's a possibility that you will achieve your goal.

Tenzin Gyatso, The Dalai Lama

Anything worth doing takes time to perfect.

Ask the great athlete or the concert pianist or the successful actor if they arrived at the place where they need no further practice. They will tell you that the higher you climb in proficiency and public acceptance, the greater the need for practice.

Eric Butterworth, minister and author

I began by doing physical yoga, initially just for the workout, as exercise. I would get peaceful and calm at the end of it, and I was curious about that ... I think we should be passionately curious about what we do. Well, I was passionately curious about what my body was doing, and when I got the lessons on how to meditate, it seemed really solid to me. It seemed real. It wasn't like, "You're going to take a weekend course and you're going to be a psychic or you can do hypnosis on your friends." It was like running a marathon. You have to train for it. You don't just go out and run a marathon or you're going to kill yourself. Life is like that. You go out every day and you put the mileage in.

Mariel Hemingway, actor

The process of becoming excellent in your field is time-consuming and painstaking.

The idea for us was to form our knowledge, to structure it, to mold it into that particular taste. It was very disciplined. If you do that for two or three years in a place like the Plaza Athenée, then you move to another place and do the same thing, after 15 or 20 years you have the accumulated knowledge of all those places and now you can filter it through your own taste, do something with it and put some more of yourself into it. But it takes that amount of time ...

Jacques Pépin, chef

People talk about, "Wow. You've had such success, and it's just been so overnight," and whatever. Well, whatever success I've got has come after like eight years of just nothing working out ...

Quentin Tarantino, film director and screenwriter

Make proper preparation. Many people hear about the idea. It is a very, very simple idea and a very logical thing. So you jump into doing it yourself, without preparing for the techniques of doing it. I would say to take that step. Prepare yourself so that you know the ins and outs of the procedures. That is number one.

Number two is start small. Don't plan for the whole country when you start out. It's a very long process. Start doing it with a few people; ten people, 20 people, and then gather experience to expand to hundreds. Gather experience to tens of thousands. Step by step you go. That is a very safe way to do it.

Muhammad Yunus, managing director and founder of Grameen Bank, a successful experiment in "microfunding" for the poor

Being an artist means not numbering and counting, but ripening like a tree, which doesn't force its sap, and stands confidently in the storms of spring, not afraid that afterward summer may not come. It does come. But it comes only to those who are patient, who are there as if eternity lay before them, so unconcernedly silent and vast. I learn it every day of my life, learn it with pain I am grateful for: patience is everything!

Rainer Maria Rilke, poet

BEING PERSISTENT

Persistence—dogged determination—is often the only trait that separates a moderately successful person from a person who is truly excellent. Persistence embodies many other qualities of excellence including risk-taking, resilience, ambition, and passion. Persistence is hard work. It requires focus and purpose. It borders on stubbornness. You have to know what you want and make a habit of pursuing it relentlessly.

Never give in. Never give in. Never give in. Never. Never. Never. Never.
Winston Churchill

Energy and persistence conquer all things.
Benjamin Franklin, founding father of the United States

I pretty much believe in that Dylan Thomas line, "Do not go gentle into that good night."
Sharon Stone, actor

Press on

Persistence requires tremendous energy, but it will almost always pay off.

Nothing in the world can take the place of persistence. Talent will not; nothing is more common than unsuccessful men with talent. Genius will not; unrewarded genius is almost a proverb. Education will not; the world is full of educated derelicts. Persistence and determination alone are omnipotent.
The slogan "press on" has solved and always will solve the problems of the human race.
Calvin Coolidge, US president 1923–1929

Hard work certainly goes a long way. These days, a lot of people work hard, so you have to make sure you work even harder and really dedicate yourself to what you are doing and setting out to achieve.
Lakshmi Mittal, chairman and CEO of the Mittal Steel Company NV

I know a very old, time-tested recipe for success. Our ancestors came up with it hundreds of years ago: "Diligence is the mother of success." I am sure that remains relevant today.
Vladimir Putin, president of the Russian Federation

Thomas Edison tried thousands of filaments to get his light bulb to work and none of them worked. And he easily could have said, "I guess all those skeptics who said that a practical light bulb was impossible were right." Obviously he didn't do that. You know the rest of the story.
Raymond Kurzweil, artificial intelligence pioneer

Diamonds are nothing more than chunks of coal that stuck to their jobs.
Malcolm Stevenson Forbes, publisher of Forbes magazine

Develop stamina

Knowing what you want and pursuing it requires you to dredge up everything in your character.

You have to stand up for what you believe. If you have to do it through whatever confirmation of personality resources you have, anger is one of them. Edge and steel are effective.
Harrison Ford, actor

You have to fight for everything—for power, for position, whatever you want to achieve.
Isabelle Huppert, actor

You have to have a plan. You have to stick with it. You have to modify it at times, but every day you've got to get up and play hard. Jack [Welch] used to see me running around, even after he left, and he'd say to me, "Remember, it's a marathon. Ten years. Fifteen years. You've got to get up every day with a new idea, a new spin, and you've got to bring it in here every day." I always kind of knew that, but until you're right in the middle of it, you never get it. His advice was right. It's the sustained ability to change that really counts.
Jeffrey Immelt, CEO of General Electric

I think we deserve credit for persistence and trying and also for learning about a lot of different subjects so we could put it all together. And not many people were prepared to do that. They were prepared to learn about their own part of the subject but they weren't prepared to learn about X-ray diffraction, for example, if they were biochemists. And if they were people doing X-ray diffraction then the details of the biochemistry [were]

often left to somebody else. So I think those were the two things—choosing an important problem on the one hand and really sticking to it and going at if from many points of view.
Francis Crick, physicist, molecular biologist, co-discoverer of DNA,
Nobel Laureate in Physiology and Medicine

Pain is temporary. It may last a minute, or an hour, or a day, or a year, but eventually it will subside and something else will take its place. If I quit, however, it lasts forever.
Lance Armstrong, cyclist and seven-times winner of the Tour de France

Always be striving for something

The most successful people always have a goal in mind and are constantly working toward it in one way or another.

I tell you that as long as I can conceive something better than myself I cannot be easy unless I am striving to bring it into existence or clearing the way for it.
George Bernard Shaw, playwright

If you want to find a reason why something will not work, you can find a hundred reasons. If you want to find ideas that work, you'll look through a hundred and find three that work.
Srinivasan Ramani, director of the Hewlett Packard research lab in India

I don't think I have reached a plateau. I have just reached the level where I am today. But I need to go above it.
David Beckham, footballer

If you believe that some day it's going to happen, some day it probably will happen. You just have to make sure you're there when it's happening, and ideally you're at the front of the parade, and the principal beneficiary of when it happens, but it's not a kind of thing where you just sort of sit back and wait.

Steve Case, *co-founder, CEO and chairman of America Online*

Focus

Develop your ability to concentrate. Focus on your goal. Envision yourself having already achieved it. Be grounded.

I don't care how much power, brilliance or energy you have, if you don't harness it and focus it on a specific target, and hold it there you're never going to accomplish as much as your ability warrants.

Zig Ziglar, *motivational speaker*

The biggest thing [Frida] brought into my life was this peacefulness. I still get passionate about things, but my passion is not so scattered and it's not needy. It's a lot more powerful because it comes with this groundedness and peacefulness ... It's about the process, not about the results.

Salma Hayek, *actor*

I believe the true road to pre-eminent success in any line is to make yourself master in that line. I have no faith in the policy of scattering one's resources, and in my experience I have rarely if ever met a man who achieved pre-eminence in money making—certainly never one in manufacturing— who was interested in many concerns.

Andrew Carnegie, *industrialist and philanthropist*

BEING PROACTIVE

Try to predict what might happen in your life tomorrow. What about next week? Next month? Next year? What might your career look like? What might be happening in the world at large, and how will that affect you? If you're proactive, you can respond to changes before they happen. You can maximize opportunities. You can place yourself in the best position possible for excellence.

Focus clearly on what can go wrong.
Benjamin S. Carson, brain surgeon

The future has already arrived. It's just not evenly distributed yet.
William Gibson, writer

Look beyond the present

It's all too easy to believe that the present will always be the same. Change is often a blind spot, especially for people who don't want change to happen.

I was reading a book recently by William Manchester called *A World Lit Only by Fire* ... It's about the Middle Ages and the transition to the Renaissance. He commented on how the revolutionary change that swept through the European world was never imagined or suspected by those in positions of leadership at the time. And he explained why. Here's what he wrote: "Like all people at all times, they were confronted each day by the present, which always arrives in a promiscuous rush with the significant, the trivial, the profound, and the fatuous, all tangled together." He went on to say that they sorted through this snarl and, being typical men in power, chose to believe what they wanted to believe, accepting whatever justified their policies and convictions, and ignoring the rest.
Al Gore, former US vice president

The great person is ahead of their time, the smart make something out of it, and the blockhead sets themselves against it.
Jean Baudrillard, philosopher

When it comes to the future, there are three kinds of people: those who let it happen, those who make it happen, and those who wonder what happened.
John M. Richardson, Jr., social and political scientist

Imagine the future

Be in the mindset of thinking ahead. It often means moving at a quicker speed than anyone else.

If you're proactive, you don't have to wait for circumstances or other people to create perspective expanding experiences. You can consciously create your own.

Stephen Covey, management consultant

Life must be understood backwards; but ... it must be lived forward.

Søren Kierkegaard, philosopher

... You have to be fully fit at the right time. Then anything is possible.

Angela Merkel, chancellor of Germany

I don't want to be left behind. In fact, I want to be here before the action starts.

Kerry Packer, Australian publishing, media and gaming tycoon

We just have to go at 100 miles an hour in all our businesses, be they television broadcasting, be they magazine publishing, be they subscription television, be they online, be they gaming. We just have to go at one hundred miles an hour.

James Packer, executive chairman of Publishing and Broadcasting Limited PBL

We call it infectious impatience ... We are trying to inculcate it in the entire organization. Infectious impatience. So that things not only get done but get done in double quick time.

Mukesh Ambani, chairman and managing director of
Reliance Industries Limited, India

Learn from the past

If it's true that the past repeats itself, examine your personal patterns. What do you need to change to succeed in the future? What opportunities would you seize if they presented themselves again?

Remember that one of the glories of being human is that we are fallible. We are the creatures who learn by making mistakes. I don't know about you, but I learn by what I do wrong, not by what I do right. An ant does not have this privilege. In ant societies if an ant deviates from the pattern that ant is a goner. Ants do not have the freedom of choice that we have.

Madeleine L'Engle, writer

The future influences the present just as much as the past.

Friedrich Nietzsche, philosopher

Everyone thinks that the past is uninteresting: It's not hot, it's not new. I love the idea of the future. But the future isn't here yet—I can't learn much from it. If you want to make good decisions about what's to come, look behind you.

Nathan Myhrvold, chief technology officer, Microsoft

BEING RESILIENT

Everyone experiences setbacks and disappointments. The possibility of failure is the flipside of taking risks. The way you respond to those failings is a good predictor of your future success. If your work is criticized, how do you respond to that criticism? If your endeavor doesn't pay off, do you quit or persist? If you've been rejected, do you despair? The following accounts are reminders that failures are lessons, too. The only thing to do is bounce back.

We are all capable of infinitely more than we believe. We are stronger and more resourceful than we know, and we can endure much more than we think we can.

David Blaine, *magician*

Our greatest glory is not in never falling, but in rising every time we fall.

Confucius

Grow a thick skin

The first line of defense against undue criticism is not to let it get to you.

I think my favorite fact about myself is that I have never been dismayed by a critic's bilge or bile, and have never once in my life asked or thanked a reviewer for a review.

Victor Nabokov, writer

The biggest mistake people make is to brood or to stew over what they imagine to have been their failures.

Mark Bennett, casting director

Rejection is an inevitable downside of the risks you must take to be excellent.

You always have to do face time, and you always have to show up. You can't be afraid of rejection, because rejection is endemic ... Every rejection is an opportunity. You have to be like a tank. If you hit a wall, you have to keep on moving to a place where there's an opening in the wall. You have to be seen ...

Lynda Obst, film producer

Without pain, there would be no suffering, without suffering we would never learn from our mistakes ... Pain and suffering is the key to all windows, without it, there is no way of life.

Angelina Jolie, actor

People who soar are those who refuse to sit back, sigh and wish things would change. They neither complain of their lot nor passively dream of some distant ship coming in. Rather, they visualize in their minds that they are not quitters; they will not allow life's circumstances to push them down and hold them under.
Charles R. Swindoll, minister

I have had all of the disadvantages required for success.
Larry Ellison, CEO of Oracle Corporation

Learn from your mistakes

Looking back on your disappointments, is there anything you can learn from them?

I'm all about learning from my mistakes.
Michael Dell, founder of Dell

Turn your wounds into wisdom. You will be wounded many times in your life. You'll make mistakes. Some people will call them failures but I have learned that failure is really God's way of saying, "Excuse me, you're moving in the wrong direction." It's just an experience, just an experience.
Oprah Winfrey, talk show host

The great Caesar, landing in Egypt, fell flat on his face on the wet shore. You can imagine the consternation of his officers, until the great and resourceful man shouted, "Africa, I've got you!" Some centuries later, the Emperor Julian, training one morning with his soldiers, lost the wicker part of his shield. He was left holding only the grip or the handle. How terrible for everybody until the emperor shouted, "What I have I hold".
Sir Vidiadhar Surajprasad (V.S.) Naipaul, writer and
Nobel Laureate in Literature

The leaders I met, whatever walk of life they were from, whatever institutions they were presiding over, always referred back to the same failure—something that happened to them that was personally difficult, even traumatic, something that made them feel that desperate sense of hitting bottom—as something they thought was almost a necessity. It's as if at that moment the iron entered their soul; that moment created the resilience that leaders need.

Warren G. Bennis, *management consultant*

Oprah's failure as an anchor became an opportunity to become a talk show host, which launched her fame.

It wasn't until I was demoted as an on-air anchor woman and thrown into the talk show arena to get rid of me, that I allowed my own truth to come through. The first day I was on the air doing my first talk show back in 1978, it felt like breathing, which is what your true passion should feel like. It should be so natural to you. And so, I took what had been a mistake, what had been perceived as a failure with my career as an anchor woman in the news business and turned it into a talk show career that's done OK for me.

Oprah Winfrey, *talk show host*

It's just a matter of reminding yourself that you're in control.

One of the traits shared ... by successful people is a sense that they make things happen, as opposed to the sense that things happen to them. The key parameter here is the locus of control. Learners who view the locus of control as lying outside of themselves often see little correlation between the choices they make and their level of achievement. When things go poorly, they blame it on bad luck or on actions of others over which they have no control. By contrast, learners with a high sense of effectiveness are likely to regard setbacks not as the immutable will of the fates but as mistakes from which they can learn and improve in the future. They study their experiences, failures as well as successes.

Richard Gunderman, *medical doctor and teacher*

Know what heals you

An effective way to bounce back from a stress, disappointment, or failure is to have a place in which to seek refuge when life gets difficult. Be aware of the antidotes for your aches and pains, and, when needed, give yourself permission to use them liberally.

I used to go in a little closet, a little tiny closet that had four barrels with some two-by-fours and a workbench on it, and just sit there and just turn the world off every time the pain came in, and go inside and just—since I was very young—just to take all the negative things and the painful things and take that and convert it into something beautiful and positive.

Quincy Jones, *musician*

When I got stuck and I didn't know what to do next, I would go out for a walk. I'd often walk down by the lake. Walking has a very good effect in that you're in this state of relaxation, but at the same time you're allowing the sub-conscious to work on you. And often if you have one particular thing buzzing in your mind then you don't need anything to write with or any desk. I'd always have a pencil and paper ready and, if I really had an idea, I'd sit down at a bench and I'd start scribbling away.

Andrew Wiles, mathematician

Occasionally, I go off for a few days just to sit somewhere on my own. I refer to it as "going into the abyss." I don't even take books because they're another way of engaging in the group consciousness. The idea is that I'll spend some time in a quite boring place where I don't know anybody and I don't speak the language.

Brian Eno, musician

Assess your stress-coping resources as meticulously as you would assess your stock.

Carol Jack Scott, medical doctor and executive coach

From the time we're born until we die, we're kept busy with artificial stuff that isn't important. Being able to escape makes it possible for me to deal with popular culture. I get some of my best work done at the ranch. When I'm in town, I sit in front of my computer, connected to the world. I need to go away in order to think.

Tom Ford, designer

Move on

Learn what you can from a disappointing experience then move on. Don't let it keep you down; don't give anybody else permission to hurt you.

When I went to the Sundance ceremony and didn't win anything for a movie I was really happy with, it made me feel bad. At that point, I decided that I was never going to give anybody permission to hurt my feelings that way again.

Quentin Tarantino, film director and screenwriter

All paths lead to the same goal: to convey to others what we are. And we must pass through solitude and difficulty, isolation and silence in order to reach forth to the enchanted place where we can dance our clumsy dance and sing our sorrowful song—but in this dance or in this song there are fulfilled the most ancient rites of our conscience in the awareness of being human and of believing in a common destiny.

Pablo Neruda, poet

BEING RESPECTED

It is often said that character is destiny. How you present yourself to the world will determine whether you're respected or reviled, honored or humiliated. Be conscious of your image. Cultivate a stellar reputation. Be identified as intelligent, witty, creative, kind. Ambition and determination won't pay off unless you're respected.

It takes 20 years to build a reputation and five minutes to ruin it. If you think about that, you'll do things differently.

Warren Buffett, *investor; chairman of Berkshire Hathaway*

Be careful what you say, and be careful what you promise, and be sure you're able to do what you say you'll do.

Willie Nelson, *singer and songwriter*

Set high standards

Set high standards for your self. At the end of the day, remember you have to face yourself.

... We're not perfect, but trying your best to be honest, fair and accurate in your life, no matter what you do and being dedicated to taking responsibility, for admitting a wrong when the train runs off the tracks, which it inevitably will, this is central to your being a person of good character. And that reputation will serve you well in business and in all aspects of your life. There is a haunting lyric in an Elton John song where he worries about being clean, and in touch with life. He laments: "I'm sleeping with myself tonight."

You will be a far happier person if you set high standards, because living up to them allows you to sleep very well every night. And that is a future you can guarantee.

Robert Kaplan, *journalist*

And at the end of your life, what do you want to be known for?

Right before he died, I asked my dad to write a letter to his grandchildren and to the great-grandchildren he would never know. I wanted him to tell them all the little things to remember, no matter how busy life got, no matter how hard things seemed.

He wrote a wonderful letter. And I want to leave you with some of his words.

"Be happy in your family life," he wrote. "Your family is the most important thing you can ever have. Be happy in your community. Charity is so important ... Character is so important. The world is always changing, and that's a good thing. It's how you carry yourself in the world that doesn't change—morality, integrity, warmth, and kindness are the same things in 1910 when I was born or in 2010 or later when you will be reading this."

William Frist, US senator

Cultivate a public image

Get a reputation that sets you apart or makes you in some way memorable and extraordinary.

There's a mystery about me because how I am in public is completely different from how I am in private. What everyone sees is really just me putting on this fun character. The best thing to do is always smile. Then nobody knows what you're thinking, and that's hot.

Paris Hilton, *heiress, actor, and model*

Never refuse to answer questions, never refuse to be photographed, and never flinch at the flashes. I shouldn't be surprised if in the next 25 years universities will offer a degree in fame.

Quentin Crisp, *actor, writer, and raconteur*

My first job was mowing lawns. I had a push mower, and I said to my father, "I could make a lot more money with a power mower." My dad was a Mr. Fix-It type, so he went into the garage and built me one—out of a little old motor, some black plywood, and a few pipes. I was embarrassed when I saw it. I thought, I can't be pushing that around. All of my friends are going to have slick-looking machines. Kids did tease me at first—until they realized that my mower could go through anything. So I got the toughest jobs in town, and suddenly I was making more money than I could count. The experience was a real lesson for me. It showed me that what counts above all is the excellence of your work.

Tom Brokaw, *former anchor, NBC Nightly News*

Respect others

It might sound terribly old-fashioned, but if you show people respect, you get respect in return.

Patrick Dunne, author and director of venture capitalists 3i

Remain service-oriented to your clients, your colleagues, and your community. Stay involved in professional and community activities. Find and take advantage of good mentors, be a good listener, tackle problems head-on and never bury your mistakes. Self-control and pleasantness always serve better. Remember your word is your bond ... As a professional, your reputation will always be your most valuable asset. I will end with a familiar theme: you have to work hard.

Harriet Miers, lawyer and White House counsel

For those to whom much is given, much is required. And when at some future date the high court of history sits in judgment on each of us, recording whether in our brief span of service we fulfilled our responsibilities to the state, our success or failure, in whatever office we hold, will be measured by the answers to four questions: First, were we truly men of courage ... Second, were we truly men of judgement ... Third, were we truly men of integrity ... Finally, were we truly men of dedication?

John F. Kennedy, US president 1961–1963

BEING A RISK-TAKER

You can't be both excellent and complacent.
Excellence requires a degree of risk—the
willingness to step outside your comfort
zone. Risk-taking embraces novelty.
It accepts uncertainty. It opens you up to
opportunities. It makes all things possible.
It energizes you. Let your curiosity and
drive prevail over your fear.

Excellence can be obtained if you:
care more than others think is wise;
risk more than others think is safe;
dream more than others think is practical;
expect more than others think is possible.
Anonymous

A ship is always safe in the harbor, but that's not what it's
meant to do.
Kate Couric, news anchor

If you have a belief, you espouse your belief. If you don't act
on it, your belief is moot.
Dave Ulrich, management consultant

The Chinese use two brush strokes to write the word "crisis."
One brush stroke stands for danger; the other for opportunity.
In a crisis, be aware of the danger—but recognize the
opportunity.
John F. Kennedy, US president 1961–1963

Accept uncertainty

Remember that nothing in life is certain. It can be a liberating thought, if you allow it.

I think the quality of a person's life is in direct proportion to the amount of uncertainty they can comfortably live with ...
Craig Hamilton, Australian broadcaster

... Rejecting the idea of certainties and needing to make the best judgments possible about probabilities, should drive you restlessly and rigorously to analyze and question whatever is before you—and to treat assertions as launching pads for analysis, not as accepted truths—in pursuit of better understanding.
Robert Rubin, financier and former US secretary of the treasury

Life is about taking a view... backing yourself. Taking the risk.
I always say, look, there are six chairs round this table.
Say there are six people sitting in them. Normally three of
those can't make a decision, two will say nothing and one will
say I'll do it. Now multiply that up to hundreds of thousands
of people. Most people don't like change, can't get their heads
round it, can't make decisions. It's about vision, isn't it?
You can't get from here to there without taking risks.
You win some, you lose some. You've got to assess the risk.
Philip Green, owner of BhS and Arcadia Group

Regard life as an experiment

Let your curiosity rather than your fear determine your actions. It's the most natural way to learn.

Try a lot of things to find all the dead ends, and learn from them.
Bill Gross, founder, Idealab

I get curious about new things, and I think I have a particular penchant: my real strength is going into a field that has not been investigated before, and finding new approaches to it. So I've applied that notion to a few of the fields that you know about. And, I guess I'm not easily inhibited by the fact that I don't know something about a subject. It doesn't stop me from dabbling in it, everybody has to learn it for the first time, so why not?
Joshua Lederberg, Nobel Laureate in Physiology and Medicine

We are taught to understand, correctly, that courage is not the absence of fear, but the capacity for action despite our fears.
John McCain, US senator

Security is mostly a superstition. It does not exist in nature. Avoiding danger is no safer in the long run than outright exposure. Life is either a daring adventure, or nothing.
Helen Keller, writer and activist

Don't be too timid and squeamish about your actions.
All life is an experiment.
Ralph Waldo Emerson, author, poet, and philosopher

Do the one thing you think you cannot do. Fail at it.
Try again. Do better the second time. The only people who
never tumble are those who never mount the high wire.
This is your moment. Own it.

Oprah Winfrey, talk show host

Taking a risk might mean stopping whatever it is you've
comfortably—and numbly—been doing.

You are all on a very elegant treadmill, from success to
success, from college to graduate school, to careers. It may
bring you immense satisfaction, but I implore you, take stock
from time to time, and if you are tempted to get off the
treadmill, then get off it. Otherwise, you're going to save up
all that frustration and have a mid-life crisis—when you're
really too old to enjoy it ...

So, have a life. Not my life, or your parents' life but your
own life. It would be great if it included some romance and
some adventure and even some failure but it should be your
own, not one you compare with the guy at the next table.

Having a life means taking some chances. From time to
time, do something that scares you. Having a life means
sharing it with those you love, of course, but also with those
you don't, because a life hoarded is a life wasted.

Bill Keller, journalist and Pulitzer Prize winner

Choose action over inaction

Taking risks requires taking action.

In life and business, there are two cardinal sins. The first is to act precipitously without thought and the second is to not act at all.
Carl Icahn, investor

Twenty years from now you will be more disappointed by
the things that you didn't do than by the ones you did do.
So throw off the bowlines. Sail away from the harbor.
Catch the trade winds in your sails. Explore. Dream. Discover.
Mark Twain

Entrepreneur Richard Branson describes a risky endeavor—a record company— that launched his career. This first success gave him momentum, and from that he started an empire.

... [Mike Oldfield] was a young artist who couldn't get any other record companies to put his music out ... he didn't have any vocals on it, and they said, "How can you ... put an album out without vocals on it?" But it was a beautiful piece of music, and we decided to form a record company to put his music out, and it was very successful. But we very quickly, you know, sort of turned ourselves upside down again and started re-investing all that money into other bands, new artists; so we [were] never ... willing to sit still.
Sir Richard Branson, founder of the Virgin brand

Minimize risks

Of course, your risks should be calculated. Risks are crucial, but only when taken meaningfully and in moderation.

I'm the last one who would actively seek out difficulties or obstacles. I try to minimize them and minimize risks. That's why I have survived everything that has come my way—disease, prison in Africa, everything imaginable that could have killed me off. Why am I still around at this age? Because, rather than searching out stupid risks, I'm considerate, professional, and good at avoiding them. And if they are unavoidable, then I assess the situation.

Werner Herzog, *film maker*

BEING UNIQUE

How do you make yourself utterly fascinating, completely indispensable, and invaluable? By being unique. Value the things about yourself that distinguish you from other people. Cultivate the abilities and traits that set you apart from others. Learn new languages. Offer new ways of approaching problems. Generate fresh one-of-a-kind ideas. Find a niche and master everything there is to know about it. Stand out. This makes you excellent.

Every man is born into the world to do something unique and something distinctive, and if he or she does not do it, it will never be done.

Benjamin E. Mays, minister and "spiritual mentor" to Martin Luther King

At bottom, every man knows well enough that he is a unique being, only once on this earth; and by no extraordinary chance will such a marvelously picturesque piece of diversity in unity as he is, ever be put together a second time.

Friedrich Nietzsche, philosopher

Don't be afraid to be different

Being unique requires self-confidence. It may be easier to do what everyone else is doing, but that doesn't make you extraordinary.

The key thing is to know what you bring to the table that's absolutely unique, utterly you, and never give it up. And see how it hooks into something generous, and then give it away.
Lynda Obst, *film producer*

When you're the first person whose beliefs are different from what everyone else believes, you're basically saying, "I'm right, and everyone else is wrong." That's a very unpleasant position to be in. It's at once exhilarating and at the same time an invitation to be attacked.
Larry Ellison, *CEO of Oracle Corporation*

There is a vitality, a life force, a quickening that is translated through you into action, and there is only one of you in all time, this expression is unique, and if you block it, it will never exist through any other medium; and be lost. The world will not have it. It is not your business to determine how good it is, not how it compares with other expression ... You do not even have to believe in yourself or your work. You have to keep open ... directly to the urges that motivate you. Keep the channel open.
Martha Graham, *dancer and choreographer*

But I think it's OK for an artist to have some diversity, and that's a hard sell these days. If something's harder to market, you'll just hear, "Oh, there's no audience for it." Of course, there is. I don't see any reason why a composer can't write songs in a more or less popular idiom and also write a symphony. Plenty of people have done exactly that. If it's a hard sell, tough shit.

Joe Jackson, musician

Look at your fingers. Hold them in front of your face. Each one is crowned by an abstract design that is completely different than those of anyone in this crowd, in this country, in this world. They are a metaphor for you. Each of you is as different as your fingerprints. Why in the world should you march to any lockstep?

The lockstep is easier, but here is why you cannot march to it. Because nothing great or even good ever came of it ... And that is true of music and art and teaching and medicine. Someone sent me a T-shirt not long ago that read "Well-Behaved Women Don't Make History." They don't make good lawyers, either, or doctors or businesswomen. Imitations are redundant. Yourself is what is wanted.

Anna Quindlen, writer

That which makes you different also makes you more competitive in the 21st century.

First there are people who are really special—Michael Jordan or Barbra Streisand. Their talents can never be automated or outsourced. Second, are people who are really specialized—brain surgeons, designers, consultants or artists. Third, are people who are anchored and whose jobs have to be done in a specific location—from nurses to hairdressers to chefs—and lastly, and this is going to apply to many of us, people who are really adaptable—people can change with changing times and changing industries.

There is a much better chance that you will make yourself special, specialized or adaptable, a much better chance that you will bring that something extra, what Dan Pink called "a sense of curiosity, aesthetics, and … joyfulness" to your work, if do you what you love and love what you do.

Thomas Friedman, *journalist and three-times winner of the Pulitzer Prize*

Take control of your own life story.

Of course, you're general, but you're also specific. A citizen and a person, and the person you are is like nobody else on the planet. Nobody has the exact memory that you have. What is now known is not all what you are capable of knowing. You are your own stories and therefore free to imagine and experience what it means to be human without wealth. What it feels like to be human without domination over others, without reckless arrogance, without fear of others unlike you, without rotating, rehearsing and reinventing the hatreds you learned in the sandbox. And although you don't have complete control over the narrative (no author does, I can tell you), you could nevertheless create it.

Although you will never fully know or successfully manipulate the characters who surface or disrupt your plot, you can respect the ones who do by paying them close attention and doing them justice. The theme you choose may change or simply elude you, but being your own story means you can always choose the tone. It also means that you can invent the language to say who you are and what you mean.

Toni Morrison, *writer*

Find a niche

Ask yourself, 'What can I do that can't easily be replicated?'

I feel very much that if I'm writing a novel, I have to offer an experience that cannot be easily replicated sitting in front of a movie screen or a TV screen. I often read books that I think are perfectly all right, there's nothing wrong with them and I can't criticize them in any way other than to say that after spending five, six hours reading a particular novel, the experience is almost identical to an experience I could have had in 40 minutes watching a quality episode of a quality TV series. That might have been good enough once, but I feel it isn't now, because it's easier to watch the television. I value books that take me some place and do something to me that I can't have happen in these other contexts, and when I write a novel, I try and do that.

Kazuo Ishiguro, writer

It's OK to specialize. Become famous for what you do and know well.

There are examples of Asian American directors, such as Ang Lee and John Woo, and successful examples too. It all shows their success. I think they made the right choice in coming to Hollywood. But often, I have been asked whether I wanted to come to Hollywood myself. My answer is that I am not suitable for Hollywood. First I don't know the language. Second, the films I make are all based in China. If I come here, I can't really make the films here. I won't even be able to make a third-rate film. So I know myself, and know that I can't really be separated from the land I grew up in. I can only stay in China.

Zhang Yimou, film maker

There are essentially two possibilities. One is to be, shall we say, an average architect and do the same thing everywhere. The other is to let yourself be inspired and even changed by the unique qualities of the place where you're building. We always try to take the second approach.

Rem Koolhaas, architect

Try a new approach

Try something no-one else has tried before. That may be the first step in earning a Nobel.

… I mixed ingredients which had been considered useless to mix. If I had just applied the standards of common sense, I might have thrown them away. So why did I mix the ingredients? Probably it's because I had the room in my heart to try. As a Nobel Museum professor mentioned, I had such a playful mind.

Koichi Tanaka, Nobel Laureate in Chemistry

Lawrence Lessig devised a new way of thinking about how ideas are shared and sold in our society.

... Imagine a group of butchers who've spent their lives dealing with cut-up meat. That's the way they understand how to make money, to cut up meat and sell it in the most efficient way. And then they come across a racehorse and, of course, their first intuition is, here's a valuable resource—we'll cut it up and sell it in bits. But all of us recognize that the racehorse is more valuable without being ground into this system of butchery if it gets to be used in this different way.

And that's the way I think we should think about our culture. Their conception of how to make money off the culture is to cut it up and sell it like pieces of dead meat. And that's of course valuable for butchers, but it's not clear it's valuable for society. If all content is locked in these little separate containers and you have to seek permission to do anything with it, then a huge potential, both economic and social, will have been lost.

Lawrence Lessig, *lawyer and activist*

Being unique is a lifelong process. It's difficult to be fresh and new all the time—but it's the only way to be.

When I first started what I was doing, it was new, but it's very difficult to be new all the time. There's a point when you have to try to always be inventive—out of that you do discover things that you would never have thought possible. On the other hand, you have to build on your repertoire and make it fresh in different ways. You kind of have to juggle between these ideas of new.

Zaha Hadid, *architect*

BEING
WORLDLY

Globalization—the process by which cultures meet and influence one another on a global scale—affects everyone. Embrace it. Learn about the world on the grand scale. Take up new hobbies. Make new friends. Accept new viewpoints. Understand the big challenges that affect us today. Be aware of your place in the universe—geographically, culturally, spiritually, and temporally. And make the most of it. The awareness of the world at large will prime you for excellence.

To live effectively is to live with adequate information.
Norbert Wiener, mathematician

But if you have nothing at all to create, then perhaps
you create yourself.
Carl Jung, founder of analytical psychology

Well, I'm a workaholic and a compulsive reader.
There you have it.
E. O. Wilson, biologist

Be a lifelong learner

The more you learn, the more versatile you'll be, and the more opportunities there will be on offer for you.

I hope that each and every one of you remembers Galileo. Not necessarily his lectures, but his lessons and his life. For as grand as all of Galileo's discoveries and contributions were, I think his example —what motivated him to live his life he way he did— was really quite simple. He was committed to lifelong learning.
Daniel S. Goldin, *former director of NASA*

I'm still learning every day from everybody. I'm never satisfied, and with this attitude I pay attention to everything.
Renzo Rosso, *designer; creator of the Diesel brand*

Most people leave college in their early twenties, and that ends their exposure to the academic world. To me that's a tragedy.
Malcolm Gladwell, *writer*

Education is not simply about academic achievement. As spelled out in the Universal Declaration of Human Rights, it is about understanding, tolerance and friendship, which are the basis of peace in our world. It is the fashion to refer to our age as one where all are engaged in a ratlike scurry for material gain, pushing aside such outmoded concepts as compassion and love of one's fellow human beings. Yet I see again and again proof that these concepts and others which constitute our basic humanity have the strength to overcome our less attractive qualities.
Aung San Suu Kyi, *leader of the National League for Democracy in Myanmar, and Nobel Peace Prize Laureate*

It is books that are the key to the wide world; if you can't do anything else, read all that you can.
Jane Hamilton, *writer*

It has always seemed strange to me that in our endless discussions about education so little stress is laid on the pleasure of becoming an educated person, the enormous interest it adds to life. To be able to be caught up into the world of thought—that is to be educated.

Edith Hamilton, *classicist, educator, and writer*

... The thing I learned most at Harvard was how to learn. College teaches you that if you want to learn about something, it's not just a thought that ends there: It leads to who to call and how to have the courage to know that you're bright enough to talk to someone you really admire—to ask them questions, to not feel like a moron, and to seek out whatever information you want. That was really great.

Natalie Portman, *actor*

I would urge you to be as imprudent as you dare. BE BOLD, BE BOLD, BE BOLD. Keep on reading. (Poetry. And novels from 1700 to 1940.) Lay off the television. And, remember when you hear yourself saying one day that you don't have time any more to read—or listen to music, or look at painting, or go to the movies, or do whatever feeds you head now— then you're getting old. That means they got to you, after all.

Barbara Bush, *former US first lady*

... If I show up at your house ten years from now and find nothing in your living room but *The Reader's Digest*, nothing on your bedroom night table but the newest Dan Brown novel, and nothing in your bathroom but Jokes for the John, I'll chase you down to the end of your driveway and back, screaming, "Where are your books? ... Why are you living on the intellectual equivalent of Kraft Macaroni and Cheese?" I sound like I'm joking about this, but I'm not ...Try to remember there's more to life than Vin Diesel and Tom Cruise. It wouldn't kill you to go to a movie once a month that has subtitles on the bottom of the screen.

Stephen King, *writer*

Experience the world firsthand

Be adventurous. Explore the world with your own senses and create your own opinions and memories.

Apply yourself. Get all the education you can, but then ... do something. Don't just stand there, make it happen.
Lee Iacocca, *former chairman of Chrysler Corp.*

A person who has experienced something is almost always far more expert on it than are the experts. A corollary is that any process including only experts, with no contribution from those with personal experience, will probably go wrong. An extension is that our educational system is long on book learning, but short on apprenticeship. A further extension is that our social policy is long on theorists, and short on organizers. A national example: The poverty programs of the Johnson Administration were less successful than the Depression projects of the Roosevelt Administration in part because the first were mostly designed by Washington poverticians, while the second were mostly local initiatives that were given government support.

For a personal example: I wish someone had warned me that book learning, as valuable and irreplaceable as it may be, can also make you self-critical, reverential and otherwise fearful of acting.
Gloria Steinem, *journalist and activist*

International education ignites a passion for understanding other people and their perspectives. That's one important benefit to working or studying abroad—and it's essential to success in our increasingly diverse world. Students with international exposure come to understand the value of

dialogue between people from different cultures and between people with different points of view. They also gain an understanding of the importance of relationships. Relationships are the foundation for meaning and success in life. They are also the foundation for strong businesses, especially businesses that care about creating mutual benefit.
Douglas Daft, chairman and CEO of Coca-Cola

A man practices the art of adventure when he breaks the chain of routine and renews his life through reading new books, travelling to new places, making new friends, taking up new hobbies and adopting new viewpoints.
Wilfred Peterson, historian

Explore the worlds far beyond your own profession. You might find a way to make all those worlds connect.

Understand the technology, even if you're in management.
Bill Joy, co-founder of Sun Microsystems

I'm an excellent talker. I've often said that I'd like to have my own talk show—with no guests. I am also an excellent driver. I am a genius at making banana splits. This comes from a combination of natural ability and the fact that I worked at Carvel through high school. I was also a belt peddler. I was excellent at that. I was a cabdriver. I was a bartender. And I was a cleaning lady with a small specialty of Venetian blinds.
Fran Lebowitz, writer and social critic

I mean, just because you're a musician doesn't mean all your ideas are about music. So every once in a while I get an idea about plumbing, I get an idea about city government, and they come the way they come.
Jerry Garcia, musician

We are approaching a new age of synthesis. Knowledge cannot be merely a degree or a skill ... it demands a broader vision, capabilities in critical thinking and logical deduction without which we cannot have constructive progress.

Li Ka Shing, *chairman of Cheung Kong (Holdings) Limited and Hutchison Whampoa Limited*

Try, even if it doesn't come naturally.

People often think that meaningful work begins with what you're good at, where your talents are, but also I think there's value in being forced to learn something that doesn't come naturally.

Po Bronson, *writer*

Understand current events

In a swiftly changing world, political events may easily shape your life. There are those who have achieved excellence by taking a leading role on the world stage.

I don't think I made a conscious decision as a career choice. From my school days I had decided, persuaded by my parents, to prepare myself for the law. Then the Japanese occupation came and we went through three and a half years of what I would call the university of life, it was hard, it was harsh ... I was slowly coming to the conclusion that we should be governing ourselves. Anyway, then I went off to England where I spent four years, where I saw the British govern themselves and I knew that they had a very sophisticated system, very tolerant society—that was in 1946-1950 ... But their interests were Britain and how the colonies help Britain be better off. So during those critical years we met amongst ourselves, the Singaporean and Malaysian students studying there, and decided that we should really come back, form a group, grow into a party and struggle and fight for power.
Lee Kuan Yew, first prime minister of the Republic of Singapore

As a child, I saw the Hindu-Muslim riots in the 1940s and I know how easy it is to make people forget their reasoning and the understanding of the basic plurality of their identities in favor of one fierce identity, whether fiercely Hindu, or fiercely Muslim. There again the appeal has to be to reason. Indeed, precisely because we have emerged from such a blood-drenched century, it is extraordinarily important to fight for reason —to celebrate it, to defend it, and to help expand its reach.
Amartya Sen, economist

The master in the art of living makes little distinction between his work and his play, his labor and his leisure, his mind and his body, his education and his recreation, his love and his religion. He hardly knows which is which. He simply pursues his vision of excellence in whatever he does, leaving others to decide whether he is working or playing. To him he is always doing both.

Zen Buddhist text

Selected Sources

BEING AMBITIOUS

Leider: Leider, Richard, "Are You Deciding On Purpose?", interview by Alan Webber, *Fast Company*, January 1998.

Waldroop: Waldroop, James, "Is Your Job Your Calling?" interview by Alan Webber, *Fast Company*, January 1998.

Tutu: Tutu, Desmond. Commencement address, Brandeis University, Waltham, MA, May 21, 2000.

Coffman: Coffman, Vance D. Commencement address, Texas A&M University, College Coffman, Vance Station, TX, May 14, 2004.

Brin: Brin, Sergey and Page, Larry, "The Google Guys" interview by David Sheff, *Playboy*, September 2004.

Lauper: Lauper, Cyndi, "Cyndi Lauper: two decades after blazing the way for a generation of female pop singers, the original day-glo diva is reigniting her career," interview by Evelyn McDonnell, *Interview*, December 2003.

BEING COMMUNICATIVE

Quattrone: Quattrone, Frank "Training to Work", Jill Rosenfeld, *Fast Company*, July 2000.

Collins: Collins, Phil, interview by David Sheff, *Playboy*, October 1986.

Auletta: Auletta, Ken, "Morning Rush," interview by Daniel Cappello, *New Yorker Online Only*, August 8, 2005.

Sinatra: Sinatra, Frank, interview by Lawrence Grobel, *Playboy*, February 1963.

Björk: Björk, interview by Juergen Teller, *Index Magazine*, July 2001.

Gilliam: Gilliam, Terry, interview by Ella Christopherson, *Index Magazine*, May 2005.

Collins: Collins, Jim, "Good to Great," *Fast Company*, September 2001.

Seely Brown: Seely Brown, John, "Storytelling: Passport to Success in the 21st Century" interview by Seth Kahan. http://www.johnseelybrown.com/seth_int.html

Warner: Warner, Mark, Commencement address, George Washington University, Washington DC, May 18, 2003.

Khan: Aga Khan, Commencement address, Massachusetts Institute of Technology, Boston, MA. May 27, 1994.

McLuhan: McLuhan, Marshall, interview by Eric Norden, *Playboy*, March 1969.

BEING CONFIDENT

Rushdie: Rushdie, Salman, Commencement address, Bard College, May 25, 1996.

Premji: Premji, Azim, "Defining moments: Azim Premji" BBC News Online, July 14, 2003. http://news.bbc.co.uk/2/hi/south_asia/3064335.stm

McCain: McCain, John, *Why Courage Matters*, New York: Random House, 2004.

Simon: Simon, Paul, interview by Tony Schwartz, *Playboy*, June 1984.

Cher: Cher, interview by Eugenie Ross-Leming and David Standish, *Playboy*, December 1988.

Robbins: Robbins, Tony, interview by Craig Hamilton, WIE Unbound, September 21, 1988. http://www.wie.org

Goldin: Goldin, Daniel, Commencement address, Massachusetts Institute of Technology, Boston, MA, June 8, 2001.

BEING CREATIVE

Fong: Choon Fong, Commencent address, National University of Singapore, Singapore, Malaysia, July 14, 2003.

Anderson: Anderson, Laurie, interview by Chuck Close, *Index Magazine*, March 2005.

Balzas: Balzas, André, interview by David Savage, *Index Magazine*, March 1999.

Resnick: Resnick, Mitchel, "Interview with Prof. Mitchel Resnick on creativity and computational media" by Federico Casalegno, Design and Computation Group, Fall 2003. http://web.media.mit.edu/~federico/creativity/resnick/resnick_trans.htm

Dell: Dell, Michael, Commencement address, University of Texas, Austin, Texas, May 2003.

Tanaka: Tanaka, Koichi, "Special Interview with Nobel Laureate on Science for the New Century" interview by Tokindo Okada, Kyoto Shimbum, January 5, 2004.

Mizrahi: Mizrahi, Isaac, interview by Laurie Simmons, *Index Magazine*, January 1988.

Brokaw: Brokaw, Tom, Commencement address, Stanford University, Stanford, CA, June 18, 2006.

BEING DISCIPLINED

Parker: Parker, Mary Louise, interview by Justin Theroux, *Interview*, October 2005.

Obama: Obama, Barack, Commencement address, Knox University, Galesburg, Illinois, June 5, 2005

Allende: Allende, Isabel, interview by Bill Moyers, transcript of NOW series by PBS, June 13, 2003.

Brown: Brown, Dan, "Veni Vidi da Vinci," interview by David Smith, *The Guardian*, December 12, 2004.

Stephenson: Stephenson, Neal, interview by Laura Miller, Salon, April 21, 2004.
http://archive.salon.com/books/int/2004/04/21/stephenson/index_np.html

Moseley: Moseley, Jonny, Commencement address, University of California, Berkeley, CA, May 17, 2002.

BEING ETHICAL

Albright: Albright, Madeleine, Commencement address, University of California, Berkeley, CA, May 10, 2000.

Dalai Lama: Address by His Holiness the Dalai Lama, United Nations Educational, Scientific and Cultural Organization (UNESCO) Meeting, Paris, February 1999

Sulzberger: Sulzberger, Arthur Jr., Commencement address, State University of New York, New Paltz, NY, May 21, 2006.

Wolfowitz: Wolfowitz, Paul, Commencement address at the US Military Academy, West Point NY, June 2, 2001.

Greenspan: Greenspan, Alan, Commencement address, Harvard University, Boston, MA, June 17, 1999.

Ronstadt: Ronstadt, Linda, interview with Jean Vallely, *Playboy*, April 1980.

Sarandon: Sarandon, Susan, interview with Rachael Horovitz, *Index Magazine*, October 2003.

Goldberg: Goldberg, Whoopi, Commencement address, Wellesley College, June 3, 2002.

Templeton: Templeton, Sir John, "Sir John Templeton— the eternal optimist", interview with Patrick Perry, *Saturday Evening Post*, March-April 2003.

Greenspan: Greenspan, Alan, Commencement address, Harvard University, Cambridge, MA, June 17, 1999.

BEING FLEXIBLE

Lamb: Lamb, Wally, Commencement address, Connecticut College, New London, CT, June 6, 2003.

Omidyar: Omidyar, Pierre, Commencement address, Tufts University, Medford, MA, May 19, 2002.

Angelou: Angelou, Maya, *Wouldn't Take Nothing For My Journey Now*, New York: Random House, 1993.

West: West, Cornel, Commencement address, Wesleyan University, Middleton, CT, May 30, 1993.

Atwood: Atwood, Margaret, Convocation address, University of Toronto, Toronto, Canada, June 14, 1983.

Feynman: Feynman, Richard, *The Pleasure of Finding Things Out*, New York: Perseus Books, 1993.

Streisand: Streisand, Barbra, interview with Lawrence Grobel, *Playboy*, October 1977.

Bergman: Bergman, Ingmar, interview by Lawrence Grobel, *Playboy*, June 1964.

BEING HUMBLE

Wiesel: Wiesel, Elie, Commencement address, Wesleyan University, Middleton, CT, Chicago, IL, June 15, 1997.

Havel: Havel, Vaclav, Commencement address, Harvard University, Cambridge, MA, Hune 12, 1995.

McCain: McCain, John, Commencement address, The New School, New York, NY, May 19, 2006.

Ramos-Horta: Ramos-Horta, José, "Q&A", Asiasource.org, March 20, 2006.
http://www.asiasource.org/news/special_reports/horta2.cfm

Dafoe: Dafoe, Willem, interview with Justin Haythe, *Index Magazine*, May 2003.

Clooney: Clooney, George, interview with Bernard Weinraub, *Playboy*, July 2000.

BEING INCISIVE

Ailes: Ailes, Roger, "Q&A with Roger Ailes," *US News & World Report*, October 22, 2005.

Breyer: Breyer, Stephen, Commencement address, Boston College, Newton, MA, May 23, 2003.

Rehnquist: Rehnquist, William, Commencement address, George Washington University, Washington DC, May 28, 2000.

BEING INTUITIVE

Dawkins: Dawkins, Richard, *A Devil's Chaplain*, New York: Houghton Mifflin, 2003.

Baker: Baker, Russell, Commencement address, Connecticut College, New London, CT, May 27, 1995.

BEING LIKED AND LOVED

John: John, Elton, "Elton's Tip Sheet," *Interview*, October 2005.

Russo: Russo, Richard, Commencement address, Colby College, Waterville, ME, May 23, 2004.

Reich: Reich, Robert, Commencement address, Grinnell College, Grinnell, Iowa, May 20, 2002.

Halberstam: Halberstam, David, Commencement address, Tulane University, New Orleans, LA, May 17, 2003.

BEING MEANINGFUL

Nehru: Nehru, Jawahawrul, interview by Kenneth Tynan, *Playboy*, October 1963.

Kushner: Kushner, Tony, Commencement address, Vassar College, Poughkeepsie, NY, May 26, 2002.

Jackson: Jackson, Samuel L., Commencement address, Vassar College, Poughkeepsie, NY, May 23, 2004.

Obama: Obama, Barack, Commencement address, Knox University, Galesburg, Illinois, June 5, 2005

Hanks: Hanks, Tom, Commencement address, Vassar College, Poughkeepsie, NY, May 22, 2005.

Zinn: Zinn, Howard, Commencement address, Spelman College, Atlanta, GA, May 22, 2005.

Serling: Serling, Rod, Commencement address, Binghampton High School, Binghampton, NY, January 28, 1968.

Lapham: Lapham, Louis, Commencement address, St. John's College, Annapolis, MD, May 11. 2003.

Azmi: Azmi, Shabana, "Q&A", interview, AsiaSource,org, October 7, 2002.
http://www.asiasource.org/news/special_reports/azmi.cfm

Wallace: Wallace, David Foster, Commencement address, Kenyon College, Gambier, Ohio, May 21. 2005.

Gass: Gass, William, Commencement address, Washington University, St, Louis, MO, June 4, 1979.

Haddad: Haddad, Andre, "Interview: Andre Haddad" by Mark Hurst, September 29, 2004.
http://www,goodexperience.com

Groopman: Groopman, Jerome, "A Doctor's Stories," interview by Katie Bacon, Atlantic Unbound, March 8, 2000. http://www.theatlantic.com/unbound/interviews/ba2000-03-08.htm

Stallman: Stallman, Richard, "Interview with Richard Stallman—Free Software, Free Society!", IndyMedia.org, July 24, 2004. http://www.scotland.indymedia.org/newswire/display_any/266

Kurzweil: Kurzweil, Raymond, Ubiquity, January 10–17, 2006
http://www.acm.org/ubiquity

Watterson: Watterson, Bill, Commencement address, Kenyon College, Gambier, Ohio, May 20, 1990.

Roberts: Roberts, Cokie, Commencement address, Wheaton College, Norton, Massachusetts, May 20, 2006.

BEING PASSIONATE

Joel: Joel, Billy, Commencement address, Southampton College, Southampton, NY, May 21, 2000.

Cho: Cho, Margaret, "Q&A", interview, Asiasource.org, August 2000. http://www.asiasource.org/arts/Cho.cfm

Ensler: Ensler, Eve, Commencement address, Simmons College, Boston, Massachusetts, May 20, 2006.

Metheny: Metheny, Pat, Commencement address, Berklee College of Music, Boston, MA, May 12, 1996.

Jobs: Jobs, Steve, Commencement address, Stanford University, Stanford, CA, June 12, 2005.

Kurzweil: Kurzweil, Raymond, Commencement address, Worcester Polytechnic University, Worcester, MA, May 21, 2005.

Tenet: Tenet, George, Commencement address, Texas A&M University, Galveston, TX, May 14, 2004.

Krakauer: Krakauer, Jon, *Into the Wild*, New York: Macmillan, 1998.

Crosby: Crosby, David, interview, Frontline, PBS. http://www.pbs.org/wgbh/pages/frontline/shows/music/interviews/crosby.html

BEING PATIENT

Hemingway: Hemingway, Mariel, "Mariel Hemingway Moves Forward By Standing Still," interview by Dave Weich, Powell's Bookstore, Portland, OR, January 21, 2003

Pépin: Pépin, Jacques, "Jacques Pépin," interview by Dave Weich, Powell's Bookstore, Portland, OR, May 20, 2003

Yunus: Yunus, Muhammad, "Q&A", interview with Asia Source, Asiasource.org, May 2, 2000.
http://www.asiasource.org/news/special_reports/yunus.cfm

BEING PERSISTENT

Immelt: Immelt, Jeffrey, interview by John Byrne, *Fast Company*, July 2005.

Crick: Crick, Francis, interview, Access Excellence: National Health Museum, Carolina Biological Supply Company, 1989.
http://www.accessexcellence.org/AE/AEC/CC/crick.html

BEING PROACTIVE

Gore: Gore, Albert, Commencement address, John Hopkins University, Baltimore, MD, May 26, 2005.

L'Engle: L'Engle, Madeleine, Commencement address, Wellesley College, Wellesley, MA, May 28, 1999.

BEING RESILIENT

Obst: Obst, Lynda, "Lynda Obst explains how to Waltz with the pythons of L.A" interview by Ingrid Sischy, Interview, March 2003.

Naipaul: Naipaul, V.S., Banquet Speech at the Nobel Banquet, Stockholm, Sweden, December 10, 2001.

Winfrey: Winfrey, Oprah, Commencement address, Wellesley College, Wellesley, MA, May 30, 1997.

Gunderman: Gunderman, Richard, "Why Do Some People Succeed Where Others Fail? Implications for Education", Radiology 2003; 226.

Jones: Jones, Quincy, interview, Academy of Achievement, Williamsburg, Virginia, June 3, 1995

Wiles: Wiles, Andrew, "Solving Fermat: Andrew Wiles," Nova Online. http://www.pbs.org/wgbh/nova/proof/wiles.html

Neruda: Neruda, Pablo, Nobel Lecture, Stockholm, Sweden, December 13, 1971

BEING RESPECTED

Kaplan: Kaplan, Robert, Commencement address, University of Illinois at Urbana-Champaign, Urbana-Champaign, Illinois, May 16, 1999.

Frist: Frist, William, Commencement address, University of Tennessee at Chatanooga, Chatanooga, TN, May 3, 1997.

Brokaw: Brokaw, Tom, "Training to Work", Jill Rosenfeld, *Fast Company*, July 2000.

Miers: Miers, Harriet, Commencement address, Pepperdine University School of Law, Malibu, CA, May 20, 2005

BEING A RISK-TAKER

Green: Green, Philip, "How I did it" interview by Sally Vincent, Guardian Unlimited, October 23, 2004. http://www.guardian.co.uk/weekend/story/0,3605,1332626,00.html

Lederberg: Lederberg, Joshua, interview by Lev Prezner, The Nobel Prize Internet Archive, March 20, 1996. http://almaz.com/nobel/medicine/lederberg-interview.html

Keller: Keller, Bill, Commencement address, Pomona University, Claremont, CA, May 19, 2002.

Herzog: Herzog, Werner, interview by Doug Aitken, *Index Magazine*, July 2004.

BEING UNIQUE

Quindlen: Quindlen, Anna, Commencement address, Mount Holyoke College, Holyoke, MA, May 23, 1999.

Friedman: Friedman, Thomas, Commencement address, Williams College, Williamstown, MA, June 5, 2005.

Morrison: Morrison, Toni, Commencement address, Wellesley College, Wellesley, MA, May 28, 2004.

Ishiguro: Ishiguro, Kazuo, "Q&A", interview by Nermeen Shaikh, Asiasource.org, Sept 14, 2004.
http://www.asiasource.org/news/special_reports/ishiguro.cfm

Yimou: Yimou, Zhang, "Q&A", interview by Barbara London, Asia Source, May 25, 2004
http://www.asiasource.org/news/special_reports/ishiguro.cfm

Lessig: Lessig, Lawrence, "Remixing Culture: An Interview with Lawrence Lessig," interview by Richard Koman, O'Reilly Network, December 24, 2005.
http://www.oreillynet.com/pub/a/policy/2005/02/24/lessig.html

Hadid: Hadid, Zaha, "Zaha Hadid: how do you answer critics who call you a diva?" interview by Rem Koolhaus, *Interview*, Feb 2005.

BEING WORLDLY

Aung San: Aung San Suu Kyi, Commencement address, Bucknell University, Lewisburg, Pennsylvania, June 12, 1999

King: King, Stephen, Commencement address, University of Maine, Orono, ME, May 7, 2005

Steinem: Steinem, Gloria, Commencement address, Hobart and William Smith Colleges, Geneva, NY, June 14, 1998.

Daft: Daft, Douglas, interview by the Institute of International Education, March 29, 2005.
http://www.iienetwork.org/?p=29253

Sen: Sen, Amartya, interview by Nermeen Shaikh, AsiaSource.org, Dec 6, 2004.
http://www.asiasource.org/news/special_reports/sen.cfm

Acknowledgments

Many thanks to Martin Liu and Pom Somkabcharti at Cyan. Thanks also to copyeditor Caroline Proud.